MW01181983

THE THRONE ROOM OF YOUR HEART

Compiled by **Shepherd's Heart Ministry**

Based on materials from
Fred Littauer's "Promise of Healing" Workshops

**Art work by Brett Payton, Patrick Craven
and P. Sullivan**

Published by Shepherd's Heart Ministry

THE THRONE ROOM OF YOUR HEART

Whoever loves me will keep my word and my Father will love him and we will come to him and make our dwelling in Him.

John 14 :21

First Printing, December 2011

Title: The Throne Room of Your Heart

Copyright 2011, Shepherd's Heart Ministry
                    P.O. Box 712, Topeka, KS   66601

Art work by Brett Payton, Patrick Craven and P. Sullivan

Cover designed by Brett Payton

All Scriptural quotations are taken from:

The Message — Remix, copyright 2003

The New American Bible, copyright 1970

New Living Translation

The Amplified Bible, Zondervan Publishing House, 1995

Names have been changed for protection and privacy.

ISBN– 13 - 978-1463772635 - (Create Space Assigned)
ISBN - 10 - 1463772637

Acknowledgements

This book would not be possible without the dedication of those who have served over the years on the Board of Directors for Shepherd's Heart Ministry. Thank you especially to those serving at the time of this book's creation and publication for their vision and support.

We want to thank those who have helped to edit and proofread, especially Venette Davis, for her willingness to listen to the Lord's direction on each detail throughout the editing process. Additionally, thanks to those many friends and family members who have encouraged and uplifted us through the planting of this ministry and the publication of this material.

Many have walked beside us in support, but those who have allowed us to walk with them on their healing journeys deserve a special expression of gratitude. They have not wavered from the daunting task of cleaning and or remodeling their own Throne Rooms and have inspired us in this ministry to reach out even more to wounded people through the publication of this material.

Finally, our most sincere expression of gratitude goes to Florence Littauer for her generous donation of material she developed in ministry with her late husband, Fred Littauer. Shepherd's Heart Ministry desires to make these materials accessible to as many readers as possible.

Profits earned from the sales of this book will
be used by Shepherd's Heart Ministry,
a 501-C3 Not-For-Profit Organization,
to provide scholarships for those needing
prayer counseling.

CONTENTS

Dedication to Fred Littauer

Shepherd's Heart Ministry would like to dedicate this work to our friend and mentor, Fred Littauer. It was through his tireless caring for the hurting and dedication to his "Promise of Healing" workshops that all of this was made possible. He touched many lives with the love of Christ so that they found hope and peace.

Most Christians who look at the career of Fred and Florence Littauer will remember the great humor of her "Personality" presentations, the heart and soul expressed in their books, and their dedication to mentor other leaders, authors, and speakers through C.L.A.S.S. (Christian Leaders, Authors and Speakers Service). Many of us cherish the time that they would spend with us who were hurting and in such need of attention. Even after hours of travel, performing or working the book tables, Fred and Florence always made time for listening to those in the body of Christ who needed lifting up or a helping hand.

Together they traveled all over the world in their ministry. I have never attended a Florence Littauer presentation where Fred was not there supporting and making sure everything went smoothly. It was when Florence was in her element on stage, delighting and edifying her audience that we would find Fred behind the scenes in his element. His element was quiet and less public, but for those of us who were part of his audience, this was a life-changing experience.

Fred was always backstage praying for some poor hurting soul, either by telephone or in some quiet corner. He was praying for them to come into a relationship of healing with our Lord Jesus Christ. No one ever did it better and more expectantly than Fred. He never asked for payment or demanded gratitude, for he knew he had been blessed richly in his life and only wanted to be used by God to pass a blessing on to others.

For those of us who were so blessed by spending time in prayer with him, we have never been the same. We treasure in our hearts his great strength of faith, his humility to search out his own healing, and his greatness of heart to share it with anyone who requested his help. He truly was a man after God's own heart and taught so many of us how to walk into the bountifulness of God's love. It is not too late to be "Touched By the Master." You will need only to take time to clean the "Throne Room of Your Heart."

.

12.

Preface

We change our hearts and our lives for the greater glory of God by the renewing of our minds (Romans 12:2).This book will help start you on that path. You will find within many tools to aid you on your journey. The majority of these tools have been tested for nearly thirty years, first in Florence and Fred Littauer's Promise of Healing Ministry and more recently, in Shepherd's Heart Ministry workshops and individual prayer sessions. We have consolidated our most successful tools into an easy to read format so others can use them to find truth and reach a deeper relationship with the Triune God: Father, Son and Holy Spirit.

This book is intended to be used as a primer or road map to set you on a journey that will take you to the very heart of Jesus. Keep it handy and use the tools often until they are as much a part of you as your arms. Keep in mind that these are only tools intended to guide you on your journey. The real purpose of any tool can be achieved only when you pick it up and put it to good use.

People today are not looking for more religion or another gimmick that offers more than it can deliver. People are hungry for a deeper spirituality and a way to renew their minds so they can finally walk in the victory that is promised in the Bible. It is through renewing our minds from the lies that bind us that we are able to walk in victory with all the passion of a grateful heart.

Chapter One
The Throne

When the Father created you, He made you in His image and breathed His life into you so that you can be a light in this world of darkness.

If you are a Christian, at some point you asked Jesus to come into your heart and take up residency there to be your Savior and King.

But like any new rulers coming into power, Jesus may need to make some changes in His Kingdom, throw out what does not work and build up what is working.

Y ou may give your life to the Lord Jesus
and say, *"Oh yes, come sit on the throne of
my heart."* But the first time something comes
along that interests you more, you may say,
*"Excuse me Lord, could you step aside a
minute so my work, my hobby, or my money
can sit on the throne and I can worship it
instead of you?"*

**For where your treasure is, there will your
heart be also.   Luke 12: 34 (NIV)**

Perhaps you ask Jesus to sit on the throne of your heart, but you never let Him do anything there.

You're out there in the world doing business as usual. In the mean time, He sits on the throne of your heart twiddling His thumbs, waiting for you to allow Him to do His job.

You vote Him in, you ask Him to be your Lord and Savior, but then you take all His power away and do everything yourself.

Or you ask Him to come in and be the King of your Heart, but then you remember how many other bad kings have sat on the throne before He came to live there.

Maybe you ask Jesus in to take His rightful place on the throne of your heart, but so much debris and trash is there from what other bad kings have left over the years that Jesus can't find the throne.

If He does find the throne, you insist He just sit on top of all the junk others have left in your heart. After all, you don't want to deal with it anyway.

But this is not just some crumbled down old king that happened to find the kingdom of your heart to rule.

This is the God of the universe who created that heart you have invited Him into so He can rule it.

This is a King who has fought long and hard just to take His rightful place in your heart. How do you Honor Him? You ask Him to sit in a dirty old Throne Room filled with bitterness, untruths, the filth of past idols, and piles of unforgiveness.

Jesus is not a King who will be satisfied with sitting on a throne that is covered by your desires for money, success, love of others or self.

"No one can serve two masters. For you will hate one and love the other, or be devoted to one and despise the other. You cannot serve both God and money.
Matthew 6:24 (NLT)

This is a King who knows what your throne and Throne Room was like when He saw it before it became defiled and desecrated by the one who rules this world with his lies and deceit.

This is a King who wants to bring your heart back to His original glory and honor.

When you asked
the Lord in to be
the King of your
heart, did you
knock a few
things off
the seat?
Or did you
go ahead
and continue
ruling your
own life,
only turning
to Him when
in desperation?

Do you once in awhile slip
into the Throne Room
to visit Him?
Perhaps you
rearrange or sort
through the boxes
of unforgiveness
in failed
relationships
that are piled
up there.

What about all the
spilt milk of
disappointments
that stained the
floor before He
got there?

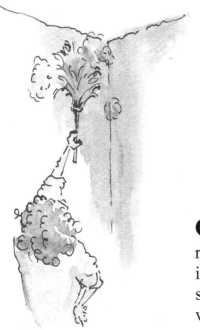

Or the cobwebs of
resentment that gathered
in the corners every time
someone came against
what your will desired?

Did you expect Jesus to just come in and clean this mess up Himself?

Or do you, like most Christians, expect Him to live with it like it is? You can't be expected to go in there and deal with the mess, can you?

And why should you? There are too many other things out in the world to take up your attention and demand your time.

So there your dear sweet Jesus lives, in the filthy, stinking Throne Room of your heart. You really don't want to acknowledge such a dirty place exists, much less go in there and clean it up.

"Woe to you, teachers of the law and Pharisees, you hypocrites! You clean the outside of the cup and dish, but inside they are full of greed and self-indulgence.
Blind Pharisee! First clean the inside of the cup and dish, and then the outside also will be clean.   Matthew 23: 25-26 (NIV)

23.

Even now you may be bringing more filth, boxes, and trash into your Throne Room. Jesus may be saying, *"Excuse me, but I live here now, and I'd appreciate if you wouldn't move that junk in here on top of me."*

So you start to change, to grow in your faith, to become the person Jesus created you to be.

You may try to paint the walls with His Word and decorate it in great stories of faith. Unfortunately, these attempts can't hide all the trash that is still there.

He went on: "What comes out of a man is what makes him 'unclean.' For from within, out of men's hearts, come evil thoughts, sexual immorality, theft, murder, adultery, greed, malice, deceit, lewdness, envy, slander, arrogance and folly. All these evils come from inside and make a man 'unclean.' "

Mark 7 v 20-23 (NIV)

24.

25.

My call is for you to look into your heart and see what you actually invited Jesus to come live with when He took up residency there.

Did you ask Him into a heart that never knew pain, resentment, bitterness, unforgiveness, anguish, anxiety, fear, or anger?

If you did, then you probably didn't need a savior and king.

Who can discern his errors?
Forgive my hidden faults?
                        Psalm 19:12 (NIV)

Or maybe the Throne Room of your heart you invited Him into needed some cleaning, sorting through, and some throwing out. He's still there in the mess waiting for your permission and help to do it.

Now you need to get some tools and go to work cleaning the Throne Room of your heart. Dare to pray that He will show you even the hidden corners of your Throne Room. Allow Him to bring it into the beauty and glory He purposed it to be when He created it.

That he may equip you with everything good for doing his will, and may he work in us what is pleasing to him, through Jesus Christ, to whom be glory for ever and ever. Amen. *Hebrews 13: 21 (NIT)*

Chapter Two
GETTING FULLY DRESSED

Normally, you do not take on a cleaning job at home in your "going to meeting clothes." You put on the clothes that fit the task at hand.

When attacking the cleaning of the Throne Room of your heart, you are wise to be properly clothed.

Being prepared and protected is essential in any battle, and cleaning the Throne Room of your heart can turn into a real battle.

> *Therefore put on the full armor of God, so that when the day of evil comes, you may be able to stand your ground, and after you have done everything, to stand. Stand firm then, with the belt of truth buckled around your waist, with the breastplate of righteousness in place, and with your feet fitted with the readiness that comes from the gospel of peace. In addition to all this, take up the shield of faith, with which you can extinguish all the flaming arrows of the evil one. Take the helmet of salvation and the sword of the Spirit, which is the word of God.*
>
> *Ephesians 6: 14-17 (NIV)*

28.

There is one who would prefer you didn't go into the Throne Room of your heart at all.

He would prefer that it remain a mess so he can use all that garbage against you.

He'll try his little tricks to block you from entering and bringing light into this darkened world.

He knows that if he can keep you in denial about the state of the Throne Room of your heart, it will remain in the dark and his plans will succeed.

You are fully armored and ready to take authority over the one who would take great delight in stopping your every move. Remember, he was rendered totally powerless at the cross of Christ.

Take up your armor and march right up there to do the work you are called to accomplish.

Use that sword to knock him out of the way. Protect yourself from the arrows of his lies with your shield. Know that when you are fully clothed in God's armor, the enemy can not harm you.

Put on the whole armor of God, that you may be able to stand against the wiles of the devil Ephesians 6: 11 (NKJV)

BREASTPLATE OF RIGHTEOUSNESS

Even if you are not wearing your Sunday best, you will want to put on a garment that will protect your tender heart from stains and rips that may result from the cleaning process.

Who knows what you will run into when you enter the Throne Room? You will surely need that extra layer of protection.

And the fruit of righteousness will be peace; and the effect of righteousness will be quietness and confidence forever.
                              Isaiah 32: 17 (NIV)

BELT OF TRUTH

For cleaning up the Throne Room, wrap that belt around you with the supplies you will need to complete the job.

You'll need the right tools for whatever mess you may encounter.

"Know the Truth and the Truth will set you free."   *John 8: 32 (NIV)*

SHOES OF PEACE

Throwing on some old boots or worn out shoes can protect your feet from wherever you might step.

If you injure your feet, how can you stand strong and finish the job?

To give light to them that sit in darkness and (in) the shadow of death, to guide our feet into the way of peace.

Luke 1: 79 (NKJV)

HELMET OF SALVATION

Covering your crowning glory is a must if you don't want to pick cobwebs or falling debris out later.

Wrap that do-rag around your glory and prepare for battle.

For the Lord takes delight in His people; He crowns the humble with salvation.

Psalm 149: 4 (NIV)

SWORD OF THE SPIRIT
The Word of God

You need to go in
with a weapon in
hand that can
tackle many jobs.

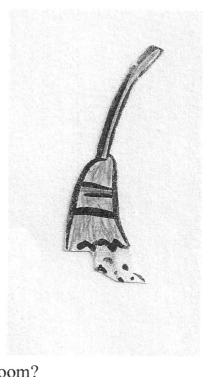

You need a sturdy
broom to attack from
ceiling to floor. Get
in there and swipe
away at what needs
to be removed.

What are the lies
and half truths you
have been believing
that need to be swept
out of your Throne Room?

*For the word of God is living and active,
sharper than any double-edged sword, it
penetrates even to dividing soul and spirit,
joints and marrow; it judges the thoughts
and attitudes of the heart.*

Hebrews 4:12 (NIV)

SHIELD OF FAITH

In your other hand is the companion tool to the sword of the Spirit. Using a dust pan protects you from having to handle all the filth your broom has collected.

You can't protect yourself too much from the contamination you may find in the Throne Room.

Take this great tool and use it to carry away all the trash and lies that have built up in your life.

Be on your guard; stand firm in the faith; be men of courage; be strong.
1 Corinthians 16:13 (NIV)

Now you are fully suited up for
battle and ready to take your stand.

*Put on the full armor of God so that you
can take your stand against the devil's
schemes. For we wrestle not against flesh
and blood, but against principalities, against
powers, against the rulers of the darkness of
this world, against spiritual wickedness in
high places.   Ephesians 6: 11 - 12 (NKJV)*

This is our spiritual clothing to wear over our spirit man. Just as we wouldn't go outside without being dressed, we also should not go into the world without dressing our spirit man.

Say this prayer at the beginning of your day. Attach getting dressed in your spiritual armor to something you do on a daily basis. Say it **out loud,** because satan can't read your mind, while taking a shower, driving to work or fixing breakfast. Continue this practice until it becomes a daily habit. Usually within a three week time period.

The Armor of God Prayer

Dear Heavenly Father,

My desire is to be strong in the Lord and in the power of His might. So in obedience to you I daily give you my mind, will, body, and emotions for your service.

Through faith in the Lord Jesus Christ, I now put on the full armor of God. I place the belt of truth around myself, taking God's truth, wisdom and discernment. I add to the belt of truth, the breastplate of righteousness which is in Christ Jesus. I place on my feet the gospel of peace shoes, and I choose to walk in your peace daily.

I take up the shield of faith knowing You are my defender. I place the helmet of salvation on my head, knowing that You give me the mind of Christ. With my right hand I take the sword of the Spirit which is the Word of God to effectively cut off the enemy.

Now Lord, I praise and thank You for the covering armor of God, and I ask You to help me be diligent and pray at all times and in all situations giving glory to God in the name of my most precious savior, Jesus Christ.   Amen

Chapter Three

TOOLS FOR YOUR BELT
NAME OF JESUS

You have a great tool hanging from your "Belt of Truth" which is truth Himself.....JESUS!

The "Name of Jesus" is like a bucket of water when it comes to cleaning.

Sprinkle it, splash it, throw it, especially at the enemy if he tries to tell you light doesn't belong in your Throne Room.

Don't let him stop you from opening that door and seeing for yourself what is in the Throne Room of your heart.

"At the name of Jesus every knee should bow, in heaven and on earth and under the earth, and every tongue confess that Jesus Christ is Lord, to the glory of God the Father. *Philippians 2: 10-11 (NIV)*

Every time the enemy pops up his evil head, throw some more water on him and drive him away.

Stand your ground in the **"Name of Jesus."** Your authority over him is in the **"Name of Jesus."**

When you command him to leave in the **"Name of Jesus,"** he has no option but to obey.

This is your Throne Room, and you've made your choice about who should sit on the throne.

Of course, the enemy won't lay down his weapons. But you will be successful if you remember to use your water to clean in the power of the **"Name of Jesus."**

So humble yourselves before God. Resist the devil, and he will flee from you.
James 4: 7 (NLT)

Suggested Prayer to Rebuke satan and Cast Him Out

In the Name of the Lord Jesus Christ, satan, I take authority over you. I rebuke you, I bind you, and I banish you.

I command you to leave this place. I command you to leave me. You are not permitted to interfere in my life.

In the name of the Lord Jesus Christ, satan, I tell you and all your evil spirits to "Be gone!" be gone from here!

After you have spoken those words, raise your hands, and looking upward, thank your Father in Heaven out loud...

Lord Jesus, I thank you for the power You have given to me over satan.

I thank You that he must obey me.

I thank You for the freedom You have given me.

Now, dear Lord, I ask that You fill me with Your Holy Spirit, fill me Lord, and give me Your Perfect Peace.

Lord Jesus, I thank you, I praise You, I worship You. Amen

Like the Name of Jesus, (pg. 40) use this prayer often and liberally just as you would use water in any cleaning job.

Say it out loud so satan can hear you since he can't read your mind. Say it preferably while standing (Ephesians 6:12). Do not hesitate to point your finger or shake your fist at him.

Say it with authority and you will drive him out of every corner in which he tries to dwell in your life.

You have no authority over him *except* in the Name of Jesus, and that authority is yours to take.

Throw the door open and let light come into the darkness.

When darkness is gone and only light is present, you will start to see the dirt that surrounds you.

You won't see everything at once. Instead, you'll notice those little stains of guilt on the walls or smears of shame streaking the floor.

CROSS OF CHRIST

Cleaning cloths can be useful tools for tackling filth and grime.

In the spiritual cleaning of your heart, the Cross of Christ can be wielded just as powerfully as you clean your Throne Room.

And having disarmed the powers and authorities, He made a public spectacle of them, triumphing over them by the cross.
1 Corinthians 2:15 (NIV)

It is your King who wants to sit on your throne, and He died on the cross for that right and privilege.

The power of the cross is right at your finger tips, just like cleaning cloths.

Place that Cross upon all areas of your life that need redemption.

By the Power of the Cross you can break down barriers, unbind and set yourself free in all those deepest areas of your heart.

Put some elbow grease behind the cross. Use it often as you would use cleaning cloths and discover for yourself what great power you have for a renewed life.

For the message of the cross is foolishness to those who are perishing, but to us who are being saved it is the power of God.

1 Corinthians 1:18 (NIV)

47.

BLOOD OF CHRIST

Just as water and cleaning cloths will go a long way in any cleaning job, the Name of Jesus and the Cross of Jesus also work wonders in your Throne Room.

Sometimes, though, you come across a really stubborn stain. Nothing will do but that super duper spray cleaner you have hanging from your tool belt, which is the precious Blood of Christ pleaded on every situation.

Whether it be a foul odor, crusted-on filth, or deeply embedded grime, pray and plead the Blood of Christ to tackle even the worst stains.

Plead the Blood of Christ for yourself often and in great love. Allow it to wash over you with its purifying freshness.

How much more will the blood of Christ, who through the eternal Spirit offered Himself without blemish to God, cleanse your conscience from dead works to serve the living God?   Hebrews 9: 14 (NKJV)

SCRUBBING IT ALL AWAY

To make the cleaning job go even more quickly and successfully, a scrub brush is a great tool to keep in your belt.

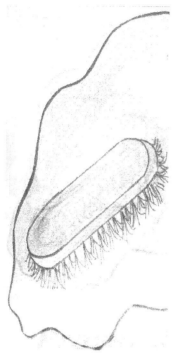

Really scrubbing away at those stains makes the cleaning seem like a breeze.

What is that scrub brush you can use when cleaning the Throne Room of your heart?

Prayer

Journaling

Therefore, prepare your minds for action; be self-controlled; set your hope fully on the grace to be given you when Jesus Christ is revealed.

1 Peter 1:13 (NIV)

51.

So often you say you are talking to your King when in reality you can't even find where He is in the mess you call your heart.

You throw a few prayers out there for Him to catch once in awhile. What you really need to do is clear out the clutter and sit down and talk to Him.

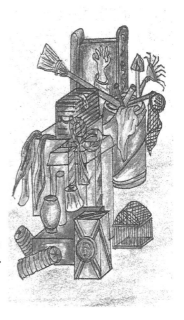

You need to write your prayers out every day to scrub away all the surface filth and get down to your real needs.

Often it takes a crisis or tragedy break open the Throne Room of your heart. You find yourself running in there to talk to the only one who can give you peace.

I call on you, O God, for you will answer me; give ear to me and hear my prayer.
                    Psalm 17:6 (NIV)

52.

Prayer Journaling can allow you to turn the knob, open the door and go into your Throne Room every day and chat with your King like a trusted friend.

Make sure you come properly dressed in your armor (see Chapter 2 "Getting Fully Dressed") . With the right clothes, you are fully coordinated from head to toe and ready to go with God to the darkest corners of your Throne Room. Clear your surroundings of anything but the presence of God by rebuking the enemy (see prayer on page 43).

Pull back the veil and let the light of God's presence fill your personal Throne Room as you read Scripture or praise Him in worship. When you sense you are in His presence, don't focus only on the surface dirt, but really dig deep and open your heart to what is hidden there.

Don't worry about anything, but in everything, by prayer and petition, with thanksgiving, present your requests to God, and the peace of God which is beyond all understanding will stand guard over your hearts and minds. *Philippines 4:6-7 (NLT)*

Thank your king, praise Him and bring your concerns right to Him so He can carry the burden for you. The Bible says that the Lord indwells the praises of His people. Let the Scripture move you out of your head and into your heart, where He dwells.

In writing your prayers, you move into the intuitive place in your mind. This allows you to tap into your heart and reveal what is really there. Write it all out as you would write to an old friend. I begin my page with "Dear Lord Jesus," as I would greet any friend in a letter.

With practice you find how easy it is to sit with your King, really open up and write out what is truly on your heart. Then you will want to hear what He has to say in response.

Write your prayers out and sit quietly to hear what He wants to say. Be sure to quiet your mind, but don't blank it out as with other practices. You want your focus to be on your Lord. Start the page with Dear _____ (place your name here) and see how it flows from His Spirit through your spirit and onto the page.

Keep a piece of scratch paper next to you. When you become distracted by worries or concerns, write them down, knowing you will deal with them later.

Don't hesitate to write down what you hear or feel He is telling you. It is important to write down the first few words you hear so He knows you are listening. Then allow the Spirit to flow with the rest of the dialogue. Let the Lord continue to scrub at who He wants you to be.

Begin by believing God will talk to you. He may give you a Scripture to look up or illuminate the Scripture you have already been reading. You may have a song spring up in your heart. Pay attention to the lyrics; this is God speaking to you. He may use impressions through your emotions or bring to your mind a poem or memory.

What you write can only come from one of three sources: yourself, the enemy, or your King.

If it is mean and cruel, it is not from the King. If it is loving and kind, it certainly is not from the enemy. And most of the time, you don't care enough for yourself to speak in a loving or kind manner.

Do you really believe in yourself enough to build yourself up or correct yourself? That is the reason for asking Jesus to sit on the throne of your heart.

If you find that your prayers are just the same day after day, try reading a Psalm to stimulate your heart.

See what line pops or jumps out at you from the pages of your Bible and write it at the top of your journal page. After you start your page with "Dear Jesus," tell Him why that line touched you and see where that leads.

Watch for images and pictures that come to your mind. These are not just your imagination. Images are the language of the heart, and God will use them to speak to you.

Don't be surprised to see Jesus in an image. He may have a special place where He would like to meet you. Stay focused on the details of the scenery and what He is telling you.

Be disciplined and consistent in this form of prayer. If you are consistent, you will find prayer, deepening as a great ocean, the intimacy of your relationship with the King. (See "Benefits of Written Prayer" page 120 in the appendix as written by Fred Littauer.)

Whoever loves me will be loved by my Father, and I will love him and show myself to him.   *John 14:21 (NIV)*

Chapter Four
TAKING OUT THE TRASH

Vows, strongholds, soul ties, bitter roots and bitter root expectancies are some of the obvious trash heaps in your life. Use the following steps for all trash removal.

First, you need to admit that they exist and be willing to name them.

Second, recognize them for the trash they are as well as the damage they are causing in the internal harmony of your life.

Third, determine that you will be freed of them totally, completely and eternally.

Fourth, be willing and committed to take whatever steps are necessary to break or destroy them.

Fifth, you must take out a specific prayer from God's armory and wield it as a weapon with no mercy for the offender.

A time to search and a time to lose. A time to keep and a time to throw away. A time to tear and a time to mend. A time to quiet and a time to speak up.
Ecclesiastes 3: 6-7 (NLT)

FORGIVENESS

One of the things you do when you clean your house every week is gathering the trash from every room for removal to the dumpster.

The trash cans in your Throne Room are filled with unforgiveness.

How many times did your family, friends, church, teachers, co-workers hurt you and you didn't forgive? Instead, you threw these hurts in a trash can with all the rest of your unforgiveness.

As you sort through and clean your Throne Room, you will run into lots of areas where you did not forgive. Keep those trash bags handy and learn a prayer to forgive from your heart.

If you forgive men when they sin against you, your Heavenly Father will also forgive you. But if you do not forgive men their sins, then your Father will not forgive your sins.
Matthew 6: 14-15 (NIV)

You can use one of many forgiveness prayers that are available, or you can pray from your heart in your own words. Remember, the key is that you <u>choose</u> to forgive. Here is one suggested prayer.

PRAYER OF FORGIVENESS

Dear Lord Jesus, I thank you that:

1) on that cruel cross You made provision for all my sins and trespasses, and that

2) when I surrendered my life to you, You forgave me of my sins and trespasses and washed my slate clean in Your eyes.

I now confess, Lord Jesus, that I have held _____ (anger, bitterness, resentment, etc.) against _____ for what he/she did or said to me. I ask You now to forgive me, Lord, for holding those feelings, and now I, at the same time, release and forgive _____ for that sin and hurt that was done to me.

I thank you, Lord, that in Your Name I am cleansed of this hurt which I have held on to for so long. I praise you for the freeing power of forgiveness. Amen.

Now that the obvious trash of unforgiveness is thrown out, it is time for you to get down to the real work at hand.

Sometimes there is so much clutter you just want to throw up your hands and walk right back out the door.

Remember that your King is right there beside you and wants to help in any way He can. He doesn't want to live with any of the clutter either.

You have to ask for His help, though, because He is a gentleman. He will not do anything against your will. He recognizes that one of the Father's greatest gifts to you is your free will.

He will not force you to choose Him. His desire is that you will use your free will to love Him above all else.

" But if you are unwilling to serve the LORD, then choose today whom you will serve. Would you prefer the gods your ancestors served beyond the Euphrates? Or will it be the gods of the Amorites in whose land you now live? But as for me and my family, we will serve the LORD."

Joshua 24: 15 (NLT)

What is the other clutter that is in the Throne Room of your Heart?

What is keeping you from worshiping your King above all else?

You may find clutter that includes strongholds, soul ties, vows, bitter-roots, and bitter-root expectancies.

You will learn how to sort these into piles and allow your King to help you remove them.

63.

WHAT IS A STRONGHOLD?

A stronghold is sometimes referred to as a soul tie. A stronghold is any "beachhead" that satan has secured in your mind and which holds you in some form of bondage or captivity from which you seem to be unable to break free. A stronghold tends to focus on a place, a thing, or an experience, and may be characterized by:

1) Any form of obsession or compulsion.

2) Any deviant behavior, or activity which you know is displeasing to the Lord, or guilt producing in yourself.

3) Any "place" that you find yourself going to, either physically or mentally, which causes you distress.

4) Disturbing pictures that occasionally or frequently cross your mind's eye.

5) Voices in your head that say you are stupid or worthless.

6) Any form of shame that lingers and resists prayer and confession.

7) Anger, bitterness, jealousy, or unforgiveness that you cannot or do not want to release.

8) Lingering dreams that cause distress and anxiety.

9) Worry, fear, depression or panic attacks.

WHAT IS A SOUL TIE?

A soul tie may be described as any illegal or inappropriate emotional or spiritual relationship or bonding with another person.

1) Any illegal sexual relationship, including but not limited to childhood abuse/interference.

2) Any illegal or inappropriate bonding relationship with another such as mother or father, counselor or counselee, pastor, etc., or strong controlling person.

3) Someone you have dreams about or wake up in the night thinking about.

4) Someone your mind continues to focus and obsess on.

5) A continuing emotional reaction to another individual (i.e. meeting them, hearing their voice on the phone, hearing their name mentioned.)

6) Someone of whom you may be emotionally afraid.

7) Someone whose name or face comes to your mind while intimate with your spouse.

8) An unborn child – miscarriage or abortion.

9) The father of an aborted child.

10) A divorced spouse.

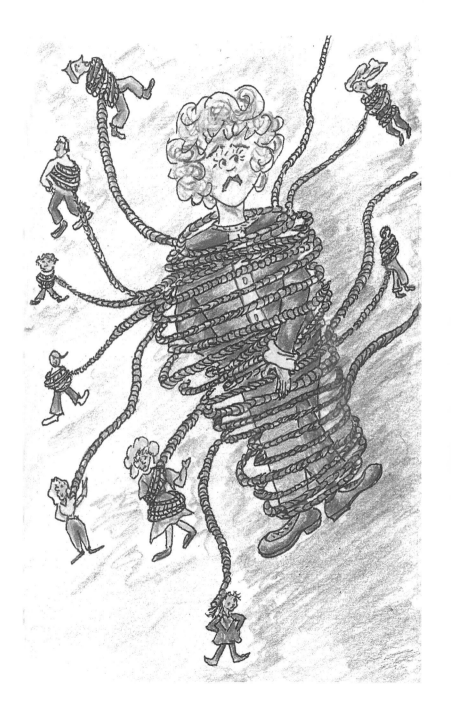

How do you break a stronghold or a soul tie?

Use the same five basic steps listed on page 58 for all trash removal. A suggested prayer to be adapted for both strongholds and soul ties is on page 68.

This prayer of spiritual authority should be repeated individually for each stronghold and soul tie you identify.

Pray the prayer as soon as you recognize the existence or possibility of a stronghold or soul tie.

Pray it out loud, as the enemy can not read your mind. Remember there is no such thing as praying too much, and you make no mistake if you pray against a condition you suspect but are not sure of. The Lord loves prayer, and satan hates it. It's that simple.

If you stumble over any words, start the prayer over from the beginning, because the enemy is only trying to stop you from being successful in saying the whole prayer.

The following prayer can help you break free of the strongholds and soul ties satan may try to establish in your mind. Select (a) the phases to pray about a stronghold or (b) the phrases to pray about a soul tie.

Dear Lord Jesus, I confess

(a)   The existence of _____, a stronghold upon my life,

(or)

(b)   That my relationship with _____ is sinful,

and I repent of it. I ask You, O Lord, to cleanse me of this unrighteousness.

In the name of the Lord Jesus Christ, I place the cross of Christ between satan and me, and I declare

(a) the stronghold of _____

(or)

(b) the soul tie with _____

to be null and void. I am cleansed by the blood of the Lord Jesus Christ, and satan, I command you to release each and every hold you have on me.

I thank You, my Lord and my God, for the power that You have given to me to break all the bondages that satan has attempted to place on me. Amen.

BITTER-ROOT JUDGMENT AND EXPECTANCY

When you judge, you set yourself up as having the qualifications and authority to pass judgment. After all, judgments are based on how you think. The conclusion you reach comes from your own opinions. When you take Christ's place as judge, you lodge a root of bitterness in your heart.

Why is this important? God says not to judge, judging sets in motion the law of reaping and sowing.

Do not judge and criticize and condemn others, so that you may not be judged and criticized and condemned yourselves. For just as you judge and criticize and condemn others, you will be judged and criticized and condemned, and in accordance with the measure you [use to] deal out to others, it will be dealt out again to you. Matthew 7:1-2 (Amplified)

Don't be misled: No one makes a fool of God. What a person plants, he will harvest. The person who plants selfishness, ignoring the needs of others—ignoring God!—harvests a crop of weeds. All he'll have to show for his life is weeds! But the one who plants in response to God, letting God's Spirit do the growth work in him, harvests a crop of real life, eternal life. Galatians 6:7-8 (NIV)

What is a bitter-root judgment and how does it operate? The term bitter-root comes from Hebrews 12:15 (NIV).

> *See to it that no one misses the grace of God and that no bitter root grows up to cause trouble and defile many.*

When you judge someone, you sow a bitter-root. A tree can only produce the kind of fruit that has been planted. What did you judge when you planted the bitter-root? This will be the fruit you will reap.

If you judged a person for being easily angered, you will reap a harvest of anger. If you judged a person for lack of self-control, you will experience problems controlling yourself.

When you judge your parents, this is doubly true. God's command is to honor your father and mother that it may go well with you (from Ephesians 6:2-3). If you judge your parents, you dishonor them, even when your judgments are true.

Bitter-roots can begin small, but the longer they go undetected and unconfessed, the larger they grow and continue to spread in your life. Just as the roots of a tree planted too close to a house can crack the foundation of the house, so bitter-root judgments grown in your hearts can crack the foundation of who you are.

Example of bitter-root judgment

Bitter-roots become woven into your beliefs, thoughts and your very identity. Take the story of Sarah.

When Sarah was 12, her father was gone during the week at summer school, and her mother was overwhelmed by being left home with four young children. Her brothers were two years and newborn. Being the oldest child, Sarah felt like she had to take on the responsibility of watching the two youngest children.

Because it was more responsibility than she was equipped for, she resented her mother and brothers for all the work she had to do. She believed that children are all work and no reward, so she made an inner vow (see page 76) never to have children.

This vow shaped her beliefs, thoughts and identity. She sought out a man who supported her in not having children. She leveraged her childlessness in building a successful career. However, she reaped what she had sown and ultimately, children came into her life.

The bitter-root had become so deeply embedded in her thinking and identity that it was difficult for her to adjust to the identity of mom. She felt pressured by all the obligations of being a parent. She felt like it was all work and no fun. Although physically she was an adult woman, her mind, will and emotions were stuck in the bitter-root judgment she made at age12.

71.

When you hold onto an ungodly judgment from your past, it tends to show itself in ungodly character traits, thinking or pervasive sin tendencies. Yes, these roots of judgment hold lies, but they are anchored by your own personal sin. In addition to judging, many times either inner vows or unforgiveness are locked in with the bitter-root.

Just exposing the lie is not enough; for the root to be destroyed, you must also confess and repent of the sin. These judgments need to be replaced by forgiveness and washed clean by the blood of Jesus that was shed on the cross. Biblical truth needs to take root where these judgments once flourished.

If you repent of the judgment but do not forgive the person you have judged, your thinking remains bent. Picture weaving a tapestry. As you weave, a small bump or warp in the weaving occurs. With each new thread that is added, the size of the flaw becomes more pronounced.

If you forgive anyone his sins, they are forgiven; if you do not forgive them, they are not forgiven." John 20:23 (NIV)

72.

When your heart is bent by unforgiveness, bitter-root judgments or inner vows, these become woven into your thinking belief system and identity. As you grow older, they will become more and more skewed, and your identity will remain rooted there until you cut off the root, repent and forgive. See the prayer on page 77 that can be adapted for bitter-root judgments and/or inner vows.

Bitter-Root Expectancy

Much like a bitter-root judgment, a bitter-root expectancy shapes your reaction and the outcome of circumstances. When you have a bitter-root expectancy, you have already determined what you think will happen. The Bible says in Proverbs 23:7, *"As a man thinks within himself, so he is."* Through your thought process, you establish preconceived notions of what will happen. Therefore, when these circumstances occur, you react to what you have programmed yourself to believe will occur through your bitter-root expectancies. What you anticipate then becomes a self-fulfilling prophecy.

Although much less powerful than a bitter-root judgment, you need to cleanse your life of the power of bitter-root expectancies. Follow the same steps outlined above to remove bitter-root judgments.

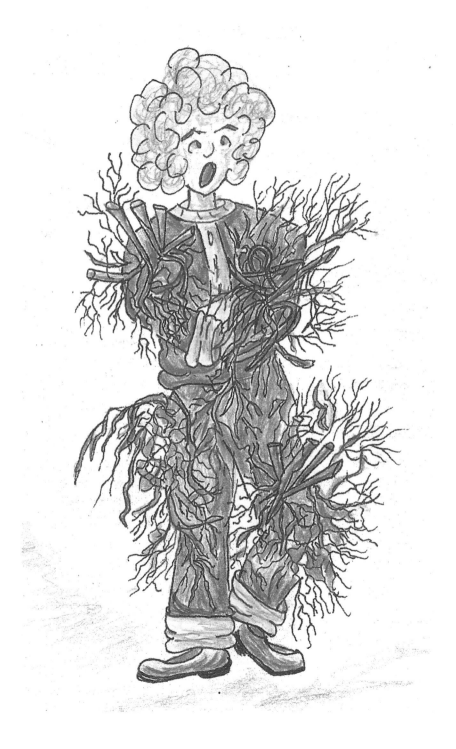

These are areas in the Throne Room that still need to be cleaned so you can have a more open room in which to meet your King.

You must confess these areas where you have judged, especially judging your parents when you were a child.

Ask the Lord to bring these areas to mind so you can take them to the cross of Christ. He died for sins such as these.

Ask the Lord Jesus to help you forgive what you judged of another.

Confess these sins to someone so they can proclaim forgiveness of the sin, *in the Name of Jesus and for the Body of Christ.*

Then ask the Lord to destroy any bitter-root expectancies in your life and bring the opposite to fulfillment.

Put to death the old expectancy and pray for the resurrection of the new expectancy.

*"Going over the past and reliving all the pain without forgiveness only reinforces it...
...Painful feelings may take time to heal, But forgiveness is a choice...and the reward is freedom."*

Dr. Neil Anderson, Released from Bondage

75.

THE CLUTTER OF INNER VOWS

You made most of your vows during your childhood. Vows can be powerful in your life because you make them with deep commitment from your heart. The enemy continues to bind you to them unless you are willing to admit they exist and confess them to the Lord.

Examples of inner vows:

I will never trust God, (men, women, friends, family... or whomever we are mad at) ...again.

I am not going to let anyone get that close so they can hurt me.

No one will ever get me to do what they want.

People in charge are mean ....I will never let anyone be in charge of me again.

An inner vow is a place where, through your own determination and hurt, you have set your heart, mind, and will. Inner vows are as vast and creative as a child's imagination.

Vows can keep you emotionally immature in many areas of your life, but become manifest in intimate personal relationships. If inner vows are guiding your life, how can you fully do God's will? For a suggestion on how to repent, see the prayer on page 77.

The following prayer can help you break free of the **inner vows** and /or **bitter-root judgments**. Select (a) the phases to pray about a bitter root judgment or (b) the phrases to pray about an inner vow.

Dear Lord Jesus, I confess

(a) **The bitter-root judgment of_____ and the expectancy of _____and I ask you to help me to forgive _____.**

(or)

(b) **The inner vow of _____, and recognize it was sinful. I repent of it and I ask You, O Lord, to cleanse me of this unrighteousness.**

In the name of the Lord Jesus Christ, I place the cross of Christ upon

(a) **the bitter-root judgment of _____ and the expectancy of _____.**

(or)

(b) **the inner vow of _____**

and I declare it to be null and void. I am cleansed by the blood of the Lord Jesus Christ, and satan, I command you to release each and every hold you have on me.

I thank You, my Lord and my God, for the power that You have given to me to destroy all bitter-root judgments (or inner vows) and ask you to give me a new heart transformed into the likeness of Christ. Amen.

Chapter Five
MEMORY BOXES

Sometimes when you start to sort through the piles of boxes that are shoved into the far corners of your Throne Room, you'll be shocked at how old their contents are.

You might be amazed that you have kept so much stored from even your early childhood. You will usually find these boxes stored in dark corners where you hope no one will notice them.

When you sort through old papers, pictures, or letters, your feelings be may stirred up like a cloud of dust. As the dust settles, look for what you really believe.

Do not be conformed to this world, but be transformed by the renewing of your mind, so that you may prove what the will of God is, that which is good and acceptable and perfect.

Romans 12:2 (NASB)

Allow Jesus to point out what is truth and what is a lie.

What is buried in all those old memory boxes that you treasure?

What false beliefs do you really keep in these darkest corners of your heart that seep out into your relationship with your King?

What is there that the enemy can use as you develop your relationships with others in your everyday life?

If you are going to truly clean all of the Throne Room of your heart, you need to allow the King to sit with you and help sort through the contents of these memory boxes.

You may discover you have to let go of many lies you kept as treasure.

Mary treasured up all these things and pondered them in her heart.
Luke 2:51 (NIV)

80.

Do, you think you know all the memories your boxes contain? On closer examination, it is not what you think that is important, but rather what you feel about these memories.

The negative emotions coming from your boxes are like two north magnets; they keep pushing you away, not allowing you to go near them. You don't want to lift the lid on all the painful emotions because they may come spilling out, invading the rest of your Throne Room and your life.

Unfortunately, all your efforts to keep these memory boxes from getting jostled around and spilling out negative feelings, require you to keep all your emotions in check – even the good ones. The memory boxes you have stored are not only bad memories. You also have good memories.

You cannot get to your cache of good emotions and good memories because memory boxes filled with pain are blocking your path.

Therefore judge nothing before the appointed time; wait till the Lord comes. He will bring to light what is hidden in darkness and will expose the motives of men's hearts. At that time each will receive his praise from God. **1 Corinthians 4:5 (NIV)**

The pain you feel when close to these memory boxes is rooted in a lie that the enemy has secretly hidden in them. That lie is so well hidden that you may not even know it exists. Still it keeps you from giving your whole heart over to the True King.

Denying that these memory boxes exist and that their lies seep into your life leaves a stench in your Throne Room. Maybe you light scented candles of worship to disguise the odor of these memory boxes, but no amount of the sweet aroma of praise to God can completely cover this foul odor.

Oh, spraying a can of prayer around will cover it for awhile ….until someone triggers a lie hidden in a box and the odor rises up again.

You exhaust yourself by continually spraying your prayers upon the stench or covering it with lighted worship candles. What you need to do is to spend time with the King and allow Him to help you sort through your boxes, find and remove the real source of the stench.

How can you truly worship and believe in His power when you do not trust Him to enter in and help you remove the real source of the stench?

Do you write great words of Scripture on these boxes and the whole area that surrounds them in the hopes it will hide the boxes enough that no one will notice them.

You continue to paint the Word of God all over these boxes. Then you sit on top of them, Bible in hand, daring anyone to pry them open.

The Word was meant to help pry the boxes open so truth can bring light to even the oldest lies stored in the memory boxes.

As you sit there spouting Scripture you have memorized in your mind, you hope no one will ever figure out that those same words have never found a home in the darkest corners of your heart.

The Word of God was never meant to hide or disguise the lies hidden in these memory boxes.

Your word is a lamp for my feet and a light for my path.
Psalm 119:105 (NIV)

You have lots of energy to keep the lid on the boxes when you are young.

Over time this becomes exhausting, especially as you mature. You find the responsibilities of family, work, church and community pull you in many directions.

With all the demands in your life, you do not have the time or energy to keep these boxes concealed. As your energy and focus are spread thin, the boxes begin to become unglued, and the foul odor seeps out into your every day walking around life.

Even though you've sprayed prayer on these boxes, lit multitudes of candles in worship, and decorated them with Scripture, the boxes are still there.

They are still taking up space in the corners of your Throne Room and infringing on space that should belong to The King.

So here's what I want you to do, God helping you: Take your everyday ordinary life—your sleeping, eating, going-to-work, and walking –around life—and place it before God as an offering.
Romans 12:1 (Message)

85.

When all else fails, you just ignore your memory boxes, pretend they don't exist get busy with anything else to help you forget them.

You set out to prove you love The King with all your good works.

You muster up your faith and go about doing great deeds.

Still, when the limelight is off of you and the applause has faded, you are left to your Throne Room. But you are not alone.

There you find the comfort of your King. He patiently sits on the boxes in the corners of your heart.

He is waiting with open arms for you to answer His call to deal with their contents.

Praise be to the God and Father of our Lord Jesus Christ, the Father of compassion and the God of all comfort, who comforts us in all our troubles.
2 Corinthians 1:3-4 (NIV)

May be you have and an incredibly strong will as a gift from the Father.

You may have learned long ago that if you really want to be rid of these pesky memory boxes and their contents, all you need to do is build walls to hide them.

You may have spent your youth adding layers of bricks to the walls. Then when you are an adult, you believe no one will ever know these boxes even exist.

These walls are your defenses so no one can discover who you truly are. They protect what you have hidden, even from yourself.

You never want the light of truth to enter these corners. You conceal your walls with great intelligence, hard work, and every mask possible to distract others from knowing what is hidden there.

Nothing in all creation is hidden from God's sight. Everything is uncovered and laid bare before the eyes of Him to whom we must give account. *Hebrews 4: 13 (NIV)*

88.

The trouble with the walls you have built in your heart is that they hide, even from yourself, those areas of your life where your King can truly be your **Savior**.

How personal a relationship can you have with Jesus if you will not even allow Him into these darkest corners of your Throne Room?

Oh, He can be your King, or God, or Redeemer. But is He truly your **Savior?** Are you willing to let Him behind the walls you have built around your heart so He can help you to find the lies that keep you from true intimacy with Him?

Intimacy isn't knowing great words of Scripture or holy prayers. Intimacy is allowing Him into even the darkest areas of your heart so that His light can purify those areas in the most need of cleaning.

He who is light will not penetrate those walls to bring intimate salvation and oneness with Him unless you invite Him to enter.

If I say, "Surely the darkness will hide me and the light become night around me," even the darkness will not be dark to you; the night will shine like the day, for darkness is as light to you. *Psalm 139 v11-12 (NIV)*

He knows how you have protected these areas of the Throne Room with all your might, and until you are willing to

Step aside,

 **pull** down the bricks,

lay down your paint brushes,

 **extinguish** your candles,

and **set** aside your spray cans,

He will not enter.

It truly is your choice. Do you want to know:

Why you have unruly behaviors
in some areas of your life;

Why sin crops up in spite of all the
seeds of Scripture you have planted;

Why the smell of
depression, discontent and fear are
able to permeate your life in times of
weakness or stress;

Why you do not feel forgiven or
worthy of receiving God's grace;

Why, after years on your faith journey, you
still do not feel you are a child of God;

Why you still believe you
have to earn God's love;

OR

Why you feel driven in your life to
prove **WHAT?**

*Instead, you
need to know in your heart of hearts
that you are greater than even the
sparrow that has every need met.*

Don't refuse to sort through and clean even the darkest corners of your heart. If you refuse, you'll miss the opportunity to know the full measure of God's redeeming love.

Allow Jesus in there to sort through your memories to reveal what is truth and what are lies.

Some of your greatest treasures have been buried by life experiences.

The pain and lies you have boxed up in your memories hide your true identity and God's unrestrained love for you.

When you remove the lies, you release your spiritual wealth and kingdom treasures.

I pray that out of his glorious riches He may strengthen you with power through His Spirit in your inner being, so that Christ may dwell in your hearts through faith. And I pray that you, being rooted and established in love, may have power, together with all the saints, to grasp how wide and long and high and deep is the love of Christ, and to know this love that surpasses knowledge-that you may be filled to the measure of all the fullness of God.   *Ephesians 3:16-19 (NIV)*

Since you have built walls to keep these memory boxes hidden and pushed to the back of the room for many years, you may need others to help you begin to honestly look at them and discern what needs to be kept and what needs to be thrown away.

Ask the Lord to bring into your life people who know how to do this sort of deep cleaning and reorganizing so that you will be able to start and complete the work you need to do.

How many of us wouldn't love a professional organizer to come in and tell us what to pitch and what to keep? Just as there are people in the world gifted in how to organize any space to be clutter-free, God has raised up some of His people to be well-versed in how to help you clear the tangle of lies that you have hidden away in your life.

Ask God to bring you people who are knowledgeable in how to bring down the walls, open the boxes, and find the lies buried there so that the **King** can reveal **His** truth.

When the lies are replaced by the One who is truth, He immerses you in His love. Then any pain that was there is completely gone as you experience the extravagant dimensions of your Savior's love.

You will begin to look around your Throne Room with new eyes.

With the Holy Spirit working deeply and gently within you, you'll have the courage to sort through the lies of your past, even those you have kept locked in such dark places that you didn't know they were there.

The warm glow of Jesus' love will light the way for you to know what is the truth and what is a lie.

When Jesus breaks the lies that have bound the spirit within you, then you discover a freedom you never knew existed.

He (Jesus) is Truth, and the Truth (Jesus) will set us free.

So if the Son sets you free you will be free indeed. *John 8:36 (NIV)*

94.

95.

What a day it will be when all the boxes and *clutter* in your Throne Room have been reorganized!

What a day when what does not belong to the *King* has been pitched, when fresh air and light pour into even the darkest corners of the room.

You will have a great view of what your Throne Room really looks like,

Once all the clutter is gone,

the keepsakes are safely stored,

the boxes organized and sorted through.

Then you will see in detail the areas that need a bit of elbow grease to make everything spic and span.

For God, who said, "Let light shine out of darkness," made His light shine in our hearts to give us the light of the knowledge of the glory of God in the face of Christ.
2 Corinthians 4:6 (NIV)

You have to remember to
wear your armor and use your
tools on a daily basis, even as
you are sorting through all this old
clutter in your heart!

Take that broom and knock
down the cobwebs of resentment
that have gathered near the ceiling.

Scrub away at the floor with
your scrub brush to break
down and remove any
stains of disappointment.

Use your cleaning cloths
and water to wash down the
walls where lies and false thinking
have left their marks.

Spray that super
duper cleaner on any
areas that remain marred from
relationships that have gone wrong.

Take your broom and dust pan and
sweep away all doubt. Your
King deserves to reside in a
Throne Room that is truly
worthy of Him.

98.

Your *King* has been there helping you with the whole cleaning process.

You are now ready for *The King* to properly reside in the Throne Room of your heart.

Run a polishing cloth over the throne and invite Him to sit in His rightful place.

Open your whole heart to invite Him in to take His place on His throne. You will be in awe at how magnificent He is. He can rule your life with all the glory you have hungered for since He created you.

AND now there is room for you to sit at His feet and learn from Him.

They will speak of the glorious splendor of your majesty, and I will meditate on your wonderful works.
Psalm 145:5 (NIV)

For many of you who have loved your King and treasured His word in your heart you may need more than just a good spring cleaning. Some of you have suffered deeper more traumatic wounds especially as a child. This last chapter is addressed to you in the hopes you will be one of the brave ones who will risk more than just a good cleaning of the Throne Room.

In the book "Living from the Heart Jesus Gave You" that was written by the staff of Shepherd's House Ministry you will find the following descriptions of trauma. With more than 30 years of experience with clients as professional Christian Counselors they have broken down trauma in the following ways:

Type A traumas are the *absence* of good things we all need. These traumas produce problems in relationships, so recovery requires a loving relationship to repair the Type A wound. Type B traumas are *bad things* that should never happen. They create fear. The "bad events" need to be revisited and the fear needs to be deactivated, so that life can proceed without fear.

Chapter Six

REMODELING WITH A PRO

I want to address you brave souls who, when you started to remove the clutter in your Throne Room, discovered the clutter was hiding more than just memory boxes or stains on the floor.

Perhaps it happened
as you dared to let
Jesus help you take
the lids off the memory
boxes.

Or when you and your
Lord took your brick
wall down.

You looked up and noticed there were cracks along the upper edges of the wall near the ceiling.

As you and Jesus moved boxes around to sort through them, you found that the paint was more than just stained. There were places where it was stripped and peeling away from the wall surface.

But everything exposed by the light becomes visible.   *Ephesians 5:13 (NIV)*

You may have begun to realize that your Throne Room needs major repairs. You need a **_Carpenter_** for your Throne Room project.

You are blessed to have right there with you the best **_Carpenter_** that ever walked the earth.

Before He became your **_Savior_** and your **_King_**, our sweet Jesus honed His skills as a **_Carpenter_** while on earth.

More tools of grace, mercy, healing and power than you can imagine are in His tool belt.

He has great skill in His role as a **_Carpenter._** He knows the right tool to use. He never uses a power tool when a light touch will do.

He always understands exactly what is needed to repair and restore your Throne Room. When He has completed this work in your heart, you realize you have been Touched by the **_Master_**.

Let us then approach the throne of grace with confidence, so that we may receive mercy and find grace to help us in our time of need.

Hebrews 4:16 (NIV)

The Carpenter can point out those places of dry rot or water seepage that are hidden from your unskilled eyes.

He will tap a little in the weakest place on the wall when it crumbles. So the truth of its decay can be seen.

When you walk across those loose floor-boards that give way and squeak, you believe you can hide them with a throw rug of denial. Only a great *Carpenter* can tell you which boards are unable to support weight and need to be removed and replaced.

Has life left gouges in the wood trim around your Throne Room doors and windows? A skilled *Carpenter* can come in and reframe the whole area if necessary, not just paint over it.

There is nothing concealed that will not be disclosed, or hidden that will not be made known.   Luke 12:2 (NIV)

Jesus will not just plaster over areas that are rotting away,

OR stick up wallpaper to hide major decay,

OR glue in pieces that need to be replaced and nailed in securely.

He will come in with His great love to repair the damage caused by the wear and tear of the world. When He finishes this working you will have a better than new Throne Room for Him to reign in.

How do you get started on your Remodeling?

Heal me, O Lord, and I will be healed; save me and I will be saved, for You are the one I praise.

Jeremiah 17:14 (NIV)

As you investigate the condition of your Throne Room more thoroughly, some of you may find there weren't just cracks, but huge holes smashed through your walls in rage or abuse.

Some may find that whole sections of wall have been ripped away by trauma you have endured, and only the inner network of studs remains intact.

As you move around your Throne Room sorting and cleaning memory boxes, you may become aware of what the boxes hid. Beneath the clutter lies shattered floor boards that have been stomped and broken through, exposing the floor joist below.

As you more closely examine the smears along the mop board, you may be shocked to discover that those dark smudges are mold resulting from the floods of tears you never dared to cry for fear of more abuse.

A bruised reed he will not break, and a smoldering wick he will not snuff out, till he leads justice to victory.
Matthew 12:20 (NIV)

Some of you may find that you need more than just a professional organizer to help you clean your Throne Room. You need a complete gutting and remodel job.

You need more than just a new paint job. You need someone who can come in and help you tear down and replace whole walls that are cracked and rotted from years of abuse.

You don't just need stains mopped off the floor. You need whole sections of floor replaced where termites of hatred have eaten away at their very core strength.

You need someone who knows how to break through the bulges in your ceilings and replace them with new flat surfaces. Otherwise, the bulges will break through and leave debris of self-condemnation all over the room.

> *Your people will rebuild the ancient ruins and will raise up the age-old foundations; you will be called Repairer of Broken Walls, Restorer of Streets with Dwelling.*
>
> *Isaiah 58:12 (NIV)*

Be willing to admit that there is real repair work that needs to be done and give Jesus permission to work. He needs to have a free hand in restoring the "Throne Room of Your Heart" as God originally created it.

Jesus will only come where He's invited. He won't force you to do anything against your will. He needs free reign and your assistance to do whatever is necessary.

You will need to work in cooperation with Him as He does these repairs. After all is finished, you will discover you are skilled yourself at finding and helping others in His Kingdom that need their own Throne Rooms restored.

What a blessing to remodel what is rightfully yours. Through hard work and teaming up with the *Carpenter*, you can do it.

> *Praise be to the God and Father of our Lord Jesus Christ, the Father of compassion and the God of all comfort, who comforts us in all our troubles, so that we can comfort those in any trouble with the comfort we ourselves have received from God.*
>
> *2 Corinthians 1:3-4 (NIV)*

Just imagine what your future maybe like if you don't do the work.

What if you never clean your Throne Room? What if that bulge in the ceiling holding back self-condemnation one day gives way?

What if the brick wall you have put up to hide your memory boxes starts to crumble and you no longer have the youthful energy to keep repairing it?

What if you continue to allow others to punch holes in your walls in fits of rage and abuse?

What if you never come out of denial and realize there are termites of hatred that have ravaged your floor joists?

What if you have given up and don't even care if the walls need painting, the windows need repaired and the doors need adjusting?

110.

Oh, sometimes you wipe the grime off windows and peek in to see if He's still in there to give you comfort.

Or you holler at Him through the boarded up door when you feel desperate.

Or at times of great loss or distress you pound on the outer wall to get His attention.

But basically, you never want to deal with the real mess in there. You're content to just forget it and pretend your Throne Room in near new condition.

The trouble, though, is that your whole life has become an empty shell of discontent, loneliness, missed opportunities, and isolation.

When you ignore the work that needs to be done on your Throne Room, you also miss the great gifts and treasures that were placed there by the King. He intended for you to use these gifts to build up His Kingdom.

Don't be left sitting alone and hopeless on the outside of your Throne Room. Resist the enemy's lies that make you feel fear, depression, distractions and being over-whelmed. You can deal with what is in there.

Take some time and ask the King to bring you into the Throne Room of your Heart. Ask Him to truly show you the condition He has been living in, perhaps since you were a small child.

112.

If you don't know how to even find the door any more, just ask your *Savior* to show you where it is.

Thrust open the door and prepare for a journey with *Him.*

Whether your Throne Room just needs a good cleaning job or completely stripped to the bare bones, your *King* will be there to walk you through every step if you will allow Him.

Find a great organizer who can help you sort through the boxes that contain lies only *Jesus* can change into truth.

Look for others who have apprenticed under the *Master* and have become skilled in helping others to restore their Throne Rooms. Allow them to connect you to the *Carpenter* for the repair work on your Throne Room.

Do not build a whole new Throne Room to false gods.

You are suppose to clean and repair the Throne Room the King created for you, the one in which He continues to dwell.

Not everyone is willing to take on the challenge of their Throne Room. But those who do will find it is a glorious place to dwell in when the world is too cold or hard to endure.

It is that place of peace and comfort where you can be with your *King*. Its condition reverberates into every aspect of your life, so it ought to be in the best condition possible.

Get in there and do your work. It will change everything in your life.

NOTES

The following excerpts are from Fred and Florence Littauer's "Promise of Healing Workshop" class material. Some material you will find in one of their many books they have written on personalities, healing or Christian living. See the bibliography for information on ordering any of these books. Material that is referenced from other sources will be listed by chapter and in the bibliography.

To contact Shepherd's Heart Ministry for copies of this book or for information on our prayer counseling services write us at:

**Shepherd's Heart Ministry
P.O. Box 712
Topeka, KS 66601**

**Or call us at
Phone 785.233.7214**

Profits earned from the sales of this book will be used by Shepherd's Heart Ministry, a 501-C3 Not-For-Profit Organization, to provide scholarships for those needing prayer counseling.

Seven Steps of Healing

John 5:

1-4	1. Realize you have a problem
5	2. Go where there is help
6	3. Desire to be healed
7	4. Express your feelings
8-9	5. Act upon the advice
10-13	6. Know who healed you
14-15	7. Testify to others

"Then I will teach transgressors your ways, and many sinners will be converted unto you."
Psalm 51:13

Synopsis of Authorities

1. Dig up the sin   Joshua 7:21-23

2. Pull up the weeds   Matthew 13 & 15

3. Roll away the stone   John 11:39-41

4. Clean the house   II Chronicles 29:5 & 16

5. Lay down the weights   Hebrews 12:1

6. Get free from the trap   Psalm 31:4

7. Wash the cup   Matthew 23:26

8. Put out the trash   1 John 1:9

9. Resettle the towns   Ezekiel 36:33-36

10. See the hidden things   Isaiah 48:6

Chapter 17
"Promise of Healing"

BENEFITS OF WRITTEN PRAYER

How can we hear the voice of the Lord if we are so caught up with our pressure-cooker lives that we leave no time to hear?

The idea of writing prayers is not new. It is, in fact, Scriptural. We have an excellent example in the Bible of written prayers. If David hadn't written his pleas, hurts, needs and rejoicings to the Lord, we would not have the Psalms today.

Oswald Chambers wrote: "A most beneficial exercise in secret prayer before the Father, is to write things down so that I see exactly what I think and want to say. Only those who have tried these ways know the ineffable benefit of such times in secret."

When we quietly take time to write our prayers to the Lord, we are also in a state of readiness to hear a word from the Lord. When the Lord does speak to us, we can immediately record in our prayer book what the Lord has said to us, even as He directed Jeremiah: "Write thee all the words that I have spoken unto thee in a book" (Jeremiah 30:2).

I do not mean to imply that everyone should write their prayers. I do, however, suggest that if your prayer life is not all you would like it to be or think it should be, you will undoubtedly find it a richer experience than you have ever thought possible.

Let us look at some blessings of written prayers.

1. *It Prepares Us to Hear the Voice of the Lord*

The Israelites sometimes heard the voice of the Lord as "powerful, full of majesty" (Psalm 29:4); at other times as "a still small voice" (1Kings 19:12); but God always spoke clearly: "Thine ears shall hear a word behind thee saying, "this is the way, walk ye in it.""...The Lord shall cause His glorious voice to be heard" (Isaiah 30:21, 30).

But who will hear the voice of the Lord? Only those who are listening: "I have spoken unto them, but they have not answered" (Jeremiah 35:17).

2. *It Enables Us to Fulfill Scripture in Our Lives*

The Lord has given us commands, directions and instructions to enable us to take on His character, to become one with Him. As we've already seen, He instructs us to "come unto me, take my yoke upon you and learn from me." Writing our prayers on a daily basis enables us to come to Him. As we voluntarily take His yoke, lay it across our shoulders and walk down life's pathway with Him, we are submitted to Him. As we daily walk with Him, since He is the leader and the one with all knowledge, we learn from Him. He teaches us something new every day, that which He wants us to learn.

In John 15:4, 5, the Lord tells us we must abide in Him, that apart from Him we can do nothing. What better way to fulfill this instruction than to come to Him daily in prayer? As we write our

121.

prayers, we are abiding in Him. Our attention is on the Lord Jesus Christ; our mind is stayed on Him.

3. *It Fixes Our Focus on Him*

"Thou wilt keep him in perfect peace whose mind is stayed on thee" (Isaiah 26:3). Many people acknowledge that their minds have a tendency to wander while they pray. That is one way the enemy detours us from keeping our focus on the Lord.

If we write our prayers, on the other hand, we are able to concentrate more effectively. When we are writing, our pen stops if our mind wanders and this quickly alerts us to refocus on the Lord. Linda Setterberg, a mother of three small children in Fairbanks, Alaska, has been regularly writing prayer and says she is able to maintain her focus and pray even while watching her children. Carol Lewis of Houston, Texas, called recently to express the great changes in her life since she started writing her prayers. "It's been so exciting. I can't believe the change in my prayer life. I have been a Christian since I was twelve, but there always seemed to be something missing. Now there is such power in my life. In the past when I prayed, it was never more than five minutes, and my mind always had a tendency to wander. Just yesterday I prayed for three hours, and the day before for one hour. It is such a powerful experience."

Writing our prayer helps us maintain an undistracted focus of devotion. The resulting benefit is that the peace of God becomes a reality.

4. *It Encourages Daily Discipline*

122.

Most of us need some form of help, especially when our lives are hectic and pressured, to bring us to our personal altar on a regular basis. How easy it is to miss a day here and there! The practice of dating our pages of prayers makes it pointedly clear when we have missed a day or two or three. We need that sense of discipline. We need a plan to help us maintain what we want to do. Resolutions are so easily made and broken.

I sometimes joke that running to airplanes is our only physical exercise. Recognizing that, I resolved in January to start a program of daily, brisk fifteen-minute walks. I did that successfully for about ten days before I missed one, then another and then another. That particular resolve needs to be totally reactivated. It has gone the way of most resolutions.

But I don't want to miss writing my prayers and spending time with the Lord in daily communion! In Matthew 6:33, we are instructed: "Seek ye first the kingdom of God, and His righteousness, and (then) all these things shall be added unto you." If we...then He! One of the clear implications of this verse is that HE must be our first priority. We need the discipline of writing our prayers to keep Him first in our hearts.

5. It Establishes a Communion With God

Commune means to have "intimate fellowship or rapport with" Does intimate fellowship describe your present prayer relationship with the Lord? If your answer is "not really," writing our your prayers could help to establish that rapport. So often we send up ten-cent prayers expecting million-dollar answers!

If we expect a return of this magnitude, we had better invest a bit more generously. As we sow, so shall we reap. If we sow little, we can expect to reap little. When we have that personal communion relationship, God becomes more real to us. He speaks to us and answers our prayer. The result is we trust Him even more and our faith in Him grows daily.

6. *It Prevents Spiritual Leakage*
Oswald Chambers writes:

> Spiritual leakage begins when we cease to lift up our eyes to Him. The leakage comes not so much through trouble...as in the imagination. It is the enemy that penetrates right into the soul and distracts the mind from God. What an enormous power there is in simple things to distract attention from God.

Having a prayer book and a place to go at the same time each day, and developing that daily discipline, frustrates the efforts of the deceiver to subtly shift our attention from the Savior.

7. *It lifts Us Out of Loneliness*
Written prayer can lift us out of our loneliness, hurt, self-pity and depression and turn us around to praise, thanksgiving and rejoicing. The basic cause of negative feelings is self-focus. Writing our prayers shifts the focus from ourselves to the Lord. The result is a switch from self-pity to an attitude of praise and thanksgiving.

Many of David's psalms are beautiful examples of what can happen when we alter our focus through written prayer. Psalm 31 is a good psalm to study. Listen as David pours out his hurts:

> Pull me out of the net they have laid for me...Have
> mercy upon me, O Lord, for I am in trouble: mine eye
> is consumed with grief...my strength faileth...my bones
> are consumed...I am forgotten as a dead man out of
> mind; I am like a broken vessel.....They took counsel
> together against me...they devised to take away my life!

After dumping all his hurt he turns his focus from
himself to his Redeemer:

> But I trusted in thee O Lord: I said thou art my
> God. My times are in Thy hand. O how great is Thy
> goodness which Thou hast laid up for them that trust
> in Thee.

Then comes the praise and rejoicing:

> Blessed be the Lord: for He hath showed me His
> marvelous kindness...O love the Lord, all ye his saints,
> for the Lord preserveth the faithful.

The next time pangs of pain and pity oppress you,
go to your prayer book and cry out secretly to God.
Continue as long as necessary until your focus turns
to His goodness. When it does, when the pain has
been cleansed away, you will rejoice with David: "O
clap your hands, all ye people; shout unto God with a
voice of triumph!" (Psalm 47:1)

As a preparation for those difficult times, get yourself into the habit of studying Psalms. See David's
true emotions being expressed and released as he
turns to the Lord for strength and salvation.

8. *It Puts on the "Full Armor of God"*

The closer you draw yourself to the Lord, the
more prone you are to the attacks and schemes of the
devil. Satan never troubles himself with those who

125.

are not abiding, but he is frustrated with those he sees slipping away from his circle of influence. Ephesians 6:12 tells us "our struggle is not against flesh and blood, but against the rulers, against the powers, against the world forces of this darkness, against the spiritual forces of wickedness" (NASB).

We need protection. We need weapons. We have the helmet of salvation on at all times, but we are told to take up the shield of faith, our defensive weapon, and the sword of the Spirit (the Word of God), our offensive weapon. Notice how the Lord, when He was attacked in the wilderness by the devil, turned the Word of God upon Satan, and said in part, "'You shall not tempt the Lord your God.'.... And the devil departed from Him until an opportune time" (Luke 4:12.13.NASB). The Lord was continually subject to attack. Are we not also?

We must put on the full armor of God daily. Is there a better way to take up our weapons for spiritual battle than to come to Him in written prayer?

9. It Strengthens Us Against Attacks

Daily prayer does not make us immune to attacks. On the contrary, we will be attacked all the more! But our daily prayer does strengthen us and keep us ready to meet those crises which can come without notice or warning. The day that starts out with beautiful sunshine may bring storm clouds in the afternoon. Tragedy, trauma and turmoil can strike at any time. We must be strengthened and prepared. Spiritual strengthening, just like physical strengthening, is a process; it takes time.

126.

Think of an army encampment in a battle zone some two hundred years ago. It is night; the troops are asleep. There are sentries posted all around to protect the perimeter. They must be alert, strong and ready. At a moment's notice they must be able to give the signal and fight any attack, any incursion or any testing for weakness by the enemy. They must be trained. They must be strong and well armed. The lives of the soldiers inside the camp depend on it.

You are the sentry who stands ready with your sword and shield. We know the enemy can never overrun the camp; he can never win. The Lord has already won the victory. But the enemy will always test us, probing for a weakness in our spiritual perimeters. Daily writing of prayers strengthens us against these inevitable attacks and crises.

10. *It Allows God to Control Our Emotions*

Emotions are God-given. Jesus, perfect man, God in the flesh, had emotions and displayed them. His emotions, however, never controlled Him. He was always in perfect communion with His Father in heaven. Though we can never be perfect, we can strive daily to become like Him, to have that mind and that attitude in us which was also in Christ Jesus (Philippians 2:5). As we commune with our Father in heaven, as Jesus Himself did, we allow Him to control our emotions, and gradually we shall become more and more like Him.

11. *It Is the Key to Our Healing and Maturing Process*

As I look back over the years I have been

coming to the Lord in written prayer, there is not a shadow of doubt that it is the one significant factor that broke the block that existed in both my own spiritual and emotional growth. Even though I had been a Christian for twenty-one years, there was something missing. I did not have a deep love relationship with the Lord and my Christian life was plagued with instability. Didn't my wife and daughter see piercing, destructive anger in me? And didn't I feel hopelessly frustrated by the deep rejection that still had a secure grip on me?

It was by being obedient, by coming to the Lord in prayer, by abiding in Him, that the branch of the vine that bore little fruit is now able to bear much fruit. I have traveled well down the road on my own journey of restoration.

12. It Deepens Love and Commitments to the Lord
God formerly was a nebulous truism, real but distant and impersonal, in my life. No longer! Because I have been faithful in coming to Him, I know Him as I never knew Him before. I trust Him. I love Him with a depth of emotion that never before existed. <u>Since I had always suppressed my painful human emotions and frustrations, I didn't even know what it meant to love Him with spiritual emotions.</u> I now understand more completely that He died on the cross for me. I have some comprehension of the physical suffering He endured so that I might have life. Something that has helped me grasp the sacrifice Jesus made on the cross is a paper written by an unknown physician titled "The Crucifixion of Jesus."

128.

It is not easy reading, but it will help you to deepen you love and commitment to your Savior. (Included in "Promise of Healing" book only.)

13. It Prevents Interference With Prayers

Do you think Satan wants you to pray? He will do everything he can to interrupt the prayers of a man or woman of God. Writing your prayers makes it that much more difficult for him to interfere.

I clearly remember one morning in September 1988. We had been back only a few day from a a ministry trip to Australia. I was sitting at my desk writing my prayers. That morning I wrote about four pages. I had prayed for quite a long time and was truly blessed and in an attitude of praise and thanksgiving. I felt led then, as I do occasionally, to read over what I had just written.

Can you guess how long it took to read over about an hour's worth of written prayer? No more than four minutes! Suddenly a question popped into my mind: *Is this the best use of your time, writing out your prayer? Think of how many more people you could pray for if you prayed orally without writing!*

That message sounded so logical, so valid, and it sounded so spiritual. "Think of how many *more* people you could pray for!" Was God displeased with me writing my prayers? Was He telling me I was wasting my time and His time, too?

Instantly the answer came to me: *No. You are not wasting your time. All the time you are writing your prayers, who are you thinking about?* At once I knew the truth. In writing, my mind was stayed on the Lord, where it should be. If I stopped writing, I would be back where I was before, easily distracted and ineffective. There was no question who had asked that spiritual-sounding question. It was satan, the prince of darkness. And the voice of the Lord was clear. It was He who gave me the answer. I thanked Him for answering both so clearly and so quickly. I have not stopped writing to Him since.

14. It Provides a Prayer Closet

The Lord specifically prescribes a prayer closet in Matthew 6:6 "But you, when you pray, enter into thy closet... pray to thy Father which is in secret; and thy Father which seeth in secret shall reward thee openly."

Where do you pray? Where is your prayer closet, where you can come personally and privately to the Lord? Corporate prayer, family prayer and couple's prayer are all valuable, but even the Lord retreated frequently into His own prayer closet in order to be alone with His Father. I once felt that corporate prayer was impersonal and generally unsatisfying. No one asked for prayer about deep personal issues. Then I realized that corporate church body prayer is not to be a substitute for personal prayer. The place for personal prayer is in one's own private prayer closet.

15. It Keeps Us Alert in Prayer

Few have ever fallen asleep while praying

aloud in a church meeting. Few have ever dozed at the dinner table while giving thanks. It is in our private prayer closet that we need help to stay alert. Colossians 4:2 tells us: "Devote yourselves to prayer, keeping alert in it with an attitude of thanksgiving." (NASB)

Many of us don't devote ourselves to prayer because we can't keep alert in it. When our minds wander, or we doze, we are dissatisfied with ourselves, as was the Lord with Peter, James and John at Gethsemane. He asked them to "tarry ye here, and watch with me" (Mathew 26:38). Three times he returned and each time found them asleep. They were not able to stay alert and keep watch with Him! Imagine His emotional pain, knowing He would soon lay down His life for His friends, His disciples—these men who could not keep awake: "What, could ye not watch with me one hour?" (Matthew 26:40). He was willing to give His life, and they could not watch one hour.

His words ring in our minds today. Can you not keep watch with Him for one hour? Can you not devote yourself to prayer, keeping alert in it? You can when you are writing your prayers. You'll be amazed how easy it is to stay alert.

16. It Refocuses What We Want From God

Our entire childhood, it seems, was focused on getting from our parents not only what we needed but also what we wanted. As we began developing a relationship with our heavenly Father, it was only natural, therefore, that our early prayers would resemble a "want list." As spiritual babes, even though we may have been physically adults, we tended to pray as children, In Jeremiah 45:4,5, the Lord says: "Seekest thou great things for thyself? Seek them not!...but thy *life* will I give unto thee."

Oswald Chambers writes:

> If you have only come the length of asking God for things, you have never come to the first strand of abandonment. "I did ask God for the Holy Spirit, but He did not give me the rest and the peace I expected." God puts His finger on the reason—you are not seeking the Lord at all, you are seeking something for yourself. When you draw near to God, you cease asking for things.... "Your Father knoweth what things ye have need of, before ye ask Him"...Then why ask? That you may get to know Him. God wants you in a closer relationship to Himself than receiving His gifts; He wants you to get to *know* Him.
>
> He is not concerned about making you blessed and happy just now; He is working out His ultimate perfection all the time... "that they may be one even as we are"...When you abandon to God, you will be the most delighted creature on earth; God has got you absolutely and has given you your life.

What is it that you want from God? Is it in line with what God wants for you? Your daily written focus on the Lord will enable you to agree with Paul, "I count all things to be loss in view of the surpassing value of *knowing Christ Jesus* my Lord...that I may know Him, and the power of His resurrection and the fellowship of His sufferings, being conformed to His death" (Philippians 3:8, 10, NASB).

Other Benefits of Written Prayer

132.

17. It Is a Written Record of what God has taught, what I have learned and where I have been.

18. *There Are Rich Re-blessings* in going back and reading past prayers.

19. *It Unleashes a Stream of Prayer Concerns.* Previously I had to think of people or things to pray for. Now they come over me like a flood.

20. *It Becomes a Bearing of Burdens* for others instead of simply "praying for others." Through written prayer the Lord revealed to me what it means to be a Simon of Cyrene, the man chosen to bear the Lord's burden.

21. *It Allows for Scriptural Confirmation of God's Responses* at a later time. One that I remember vividly happened some time ago. I was talking to the Lord about my perception that Florence was not meeting my emotional needs. He told me I was not to emphasize telling her "I love you" so that she would tell me back, but was to show her how much I loved her.

About two weeks later I was studying through 1 John. I came across a verse that I had seen many times before: "Little children, let us not love with word or tongue, but in deed and truth" (1John 3:18, NASB). I had seen that before, but I had never seen it as He revealed it to me at that moment! I was in awe of the wondrous power of the Lord, for I remembered clearly what He told me two weeks previously. In my Bible I immediately paraphrased, "Love is not

133.

an explanation, not a proclamation. Love is a demonstration."

22. *It Lifts Prayer to a Higher Plane.* I have known joy, praise, thanksgiving, spiritual emotion and ecstasy in prayer such as I never before knew could be possible.

23. *It Is the Working Out of What God Has Worked In.* Listening to a lecture on refereeing basketball does not make me a referee, any more than watching a Stormie Omartian exercise video strengthens my muscles. I have to get in there and do it myself.

24. *It Is a Deliberate Act of Worship.* The whole concept of worship has taken on a new meaning as my written prayer life develops. I worship the Lord daily. Invariably I begin my communion with Him in praise and thanksgiving, gradually drifting into other areas and returning at the conclusion to fervent expressions of love and adoration. When I sit down with prayer book in hand, I come specifically to worship Him, to exalt Hs name.

This discussion certainly does not cover all the benefits of written prayer, for the blessings and thoughts of the Lord are more in number than the sands by the sea. It is but for us to tap into that well from which springs the river of living waters.

Chapter 18
"Promise of Healing"

SOME SECRETS OF EFFECTIVE PRAYER

Prayer is the foundation of our whole Christian life. It is the way we come to our Father in heaven, to talk, to share, to commune. It is how we fulfill our Lord's instructions to abide in Him. When we pray we obey Him. When we pray we are following His example, for Jesus Himself communed regularly with His Father in heaven.

Prayer is the means of tapping into the power that is available to us. It is the method God has given us to know Him, grow in Him and develop our trust relationship.

Despite all of this, personal prayer is usually the most neglected aspect of our spiritual life. We are too busy, active or occupied to set aside time for prayer.

I remember reading a biography of Martin Luther, in which he was quoted as saying, "I have so much to do today, I could never get through it all. So I think I will spend the first three hours in prayer." At the time, I wondered how he could spend three hours in prayer. Now I understand!

We tend to relegate the discipline of prayer to either the moments when we have time (which never seems to happen), or when we are in a crisis.

Changing Your Prayer Habit
Writing our prayers is nothing more than writing

down what we would otherwise speak orally or think silently. We can also think of it as writing a daily letter to our Father in heaven. It is no more complicated than that. There are no rights or wrongs. The only "wrong" you could commit is not doing it.

Writing my prayers is the most effective way I know of going into my prayer closet to be alone and quiet with the Lord. Since the Lord generally speaks to me in a still, small voice, I allow myself to be in the position and the condition to hear His voice: writing silently with my mind focused on Him. If I were rushing around sending up "arrow prayers," it is unlikely I would ever hear His voice.

How do I know when I hear His voice? Is it audible? No. But there have been occasions when it was so clear, it could have been audible. I know that it is His voice when I am writing my prayer and a distinct godly thought comes to me. Other times, a certain Bible verse or truth comes to my mind which specifically relates to something I am talking to my Father about. I get excited when I realize the Lord has revealed His truth to me. At other times, a certain name will suddenly come to mind for whom I should intercede. Writing my prayers is a deliberate step of putting myself in a position to hear His voice.

In Luke 18:1, we read, "Then he spoke a parable to them, that men always ought to pray and not lose heart." The Lord uses a parable to show us not only that we should pray, but that we should come continually to the Father. He likes to hear from us!

Keep Journal and Prayer Notebook Separate

It's important to note that written prayer is *not* journaling. Many people who are seeking and searching for truth are in the practice of periodically writing down feelings, emotions and experiences. Journaling is a healthy and helpful exercise that enables you to keep track of various thoughts that flash into your mind.

If you journal, we strongly suggest that you use a separate book for your written prayers to enable you to keep your prayer life distinct from your journal. Those who have begun by using one book for both purposes often find they start out in prayer, but soon drift off into journaling. Journaling is helpful, but praying is *essential.*

Pray for Others

A final important part of prayer is intercessory prayer. In the words of Oswald Chambers, "Intercession means we rouse ourselves up to get the mind of Christ about the one for whom we pray." Our prayer for others focuses on knowing Christ's purpose for them. This may prove to be vastly different from our plans for them!

When to Pray

If you are going to be successful in developing a disciplined written prayer life, you will need to set aside a certain time of the day as the time you reserve for the Lord. Most people find that the first thing in the morning suits them best. This seems to be confirmed by Matthew 6:33; "Seek ye *first* the kingdom of God and His righteousness." In the early morning we are alert and fresh. Our minds have not yet been distracted by the events of the day. A young mother with little children who demand her attention first thing in the morning, or a husband who has to be on the job at 6 a.m., may find it impossible to set aside time early in the morning. That's okay. Each one of us has been given twenty-four hours in each day. Our task is to find one of those twenty-four hours to spend with Him.

There is no magic in praying for one hour. Clearly the Lord asked Peter, James and John to keep watch with Him for one hour. I personally believe He is asking that of us today as well, if we are serious about wanting to abide in Him. To become like Him, to receive His healing, we will desire to give Him one hour each day. If we give Him less, we show Him we regard Him less.

How often should we come to Him? The Scriptures give us the answer. To refer to but a few:

Psalm 61:8	I will sing praise unto thy name forever, that I may *daily* perform my vows.
Psalm 72:15	Prayer also shall be made for him continually and *daily* shall he be praised.
Psalm 88:9	Lord, I have called *daily* upon thee, I have stretched out my hands unto thee.

| Psalm 145:2 | *Every day* will I bless thee; and I will praise thy name forever and ever. |
| Luke 9:23 | If any man will come after me, let him deny himself, take up his cross *daily* and follow me. |

Writing our prayers daily comes into clear alignment with these verses. Coming before God daily helps us to deny ourselves and our personal goals, lift Him up into our lives, and follow Him.

Are you ready now to set aside one hour each day to be with the Lord? You will be tapping into a reservoir of spiritual riches whose depths will take a lifetime to discover. Don't let one more day pass without beginning this rewarding spiritual discipline.

Chapter 19
"Promise of Healing"

Prayer Starters

Often I (Fred) begin my written prayer with the word of the Lord as recorded in Matthew 11:25: "I praise Thee, O Father, Lord of heaven and earth that Thou...." and then I continue with whatever is on my heart that day. Sometimes I come to my prayer closet with needs or thoughts on my mind. Other days I have no agenda. I just start to write. Many times a verse in the Scriptures will set off my prayers.

Our recommendation to you is to start off each day by studying Oswald Chambers' thought for the day in *My Utmost for His Highest*. You will want to underline or highlight specific concepts or sentences that are significant to you. Highlighting key phrases will enable you to mine the wealth of wisdom in this outstanding book.

Following your reading in Chambers, pursue a plan of study in the Scriptures. Many types have already been suggested. We strongly recommend using the *Thompson Chain Reference Bible*. It has a wealth of additional information and resources. It is available in the *King James* or *New International* version. For my personal study, I am partial to the *New American Standard Bible*. It also contains excellent chain references, especially in the New Testament.

Having completed your study of the Scriptures, it is time to take up your pen and begin your deliberate act of worship. To assist you in beginning your own book of prayer, I have put together a list of thirty-six prayer-starter verses. Simply write out the suggested verse and then continue the thoughts expressed in the verse in your own words. For example, using Psalm 9:12 for a starter, you'd write: "I will praise thee, O Lord, with all my whole heart. I will be glad and rejoice in thee: I will sing praises to thy name" and then continue writing in your own words.

Here's how one might continue the above thought:

Lord Jesus, I thank you today for the joy of coming to You in prayer. I can't believe that you are here, hearing every beat of my heart, but I know You are. I will praise you today with my lips and my heart. You have chosen me to be Your own; I am loved. Lord, Help me to love others today the way you love me...

When ever you feel a little dry and need something to prime your pump, try one of these prayer starters:

Day:

1. "I will praise thee, O Lord, with all my whole heart. I will be glad and rejoice in thee: I will sing praises to they name" (Psalm 9:1-2).

2. "Peace I leave with you; My peace I give to you; not as the world gives, do I give to you. Let not your heart be troubled, nor let it be fearful" (John 14:27, NASB).

3. "Thou will keep him in perfect peace whose mind is stayed on Thee: because he trusteth in Thee" (Isaiah 26:3)

141.

4. "Since He Himself was tempted in that which He has suffered, He is able to come to the aid of those who are tempted" (Hebrews 2:18, NASB).

5. "Keep watching and praying, that you may not enter into temptation; the spirit is willing, but the flesh is weak" (Matthew 26:41, NASB).

6. "I have prayed for you that your faith may not fail" (Luke 22:32, NASB).

7. "God of all comfort; who comforts us in all our affliction, so that we may be able to comfort those who are in any affliction" (2 Corinthians 1: 3,4, NASB).

8. "Seek ye first the kingdom of God, and His righteousness, and all these things shall be added unto you" (Matthew 6:33).

9. "He who abides in Me, and I in him, he bears much fruit; for apart from Me you can do nothing" (John 15:5, NASB).

10. "She came and began to bow down before Him, saying, 'Lord, help me" (Matthew 15:25, NASB).

11. "Save me, O God, for the waters are coming in unto my soul. I sink in deep mire, where there is no standing: I am come into deep waters where the floods overflow me. I am weary of my crying; my throat is dried: mine eyes fail while I wait for my God" (Psalm 69: 1-3).

12. "Could ye not keep watch with Me for one hour?" (Matthew 26:40)

13. "This kind cannot come out by anything but prayer" (Mark 9:29, NASB).

14. "Although he was a son He learned

obedience from the things which He suffered" (Hebrews 5:8, NASB).

15. "I praise Thee, O Father, Lord of heaven and earth" (Luke 10:21, NASB).

16. "Whatever is true, whatever is honorable, whatever is right, whatever is pure, whatever is lovely, whatever is of good repute, if there is any   excellence and if anything worthy of praise, let your mind dwell on these things" (Philippians 4:8, NASB).

17. "Always giving thanks for all things in the name of our Lord Jesus Christ" (Ephesians 5:20, NASB).

18. "And the Lord turned the captivity of Job, when he prayed for his friends" (Job 42:10).

19. "You, too, now have sorrow, but I will see you again, and your heart will rejoice, and no one takes your joy away from you" (John 16:22, NASB).

20. "I do not ask on behalf of these alone, but for those also who believe in me" (John 17:20).

21. "Truly, truly, I say to you, that you will weep and lament...but your sorrow will be turned to joy" (John 16:20, NASB).

22. "We do not lose heart...our inner man is being renewed day by day" (2 Corinthians 4:16, NASB).

23. "Not one of us lives for himself...we live for the Lord...whether we live or die; we are the Lord's" (Romans 14:7,8, NASB).

24. "We who are strong ought to bear the weaknesses of those without strength, and not just please ourselves...for even Christ did not please

143.

Himself" (Romans 15: 1,3, NASB).

25. "You shall love the Lord your God with all your heart, with all your soul, and with all your mind" (Matthew 22:37, NASB).

26. "For we are His workmanship, created in Christ Jesus for good works, which God prepared beforehand, that we should walk in them" (Ephesians 2:10, NASB).

27. "He rejoiced greatly in the Holy Spirit, and said, 'I praise Thee, O Father, Lord of Heaven and earth'" (Luke 10:21,NASB).

28. "Enter into His gates with thanksgiving, and into His courts with praise, be thankful unto Him, and bless His name" (Psalm 100:4).

29. "I count all things to be loss in view of the surpassing value of knowing Christ Jesus my Lord" (Philippians 3:8, NASB).

30. "Come to Me all who are weary and heavy laden, and I will give you rest. Take My yoke upon you, and learn from Me...and you shall find rest for your souls" (Matthew 11:28, 29, NASB).

31. "Now that you know this truth, how happy you will be if you put it into practice" (John 13:17, TEV).

32. "Without faith it is impossible to please Him, for He that cometh to God must believe that He is and that He is a rewarder of them that diligently seek Him" (Hebrews 11:6).

33. "O God, thou knowest my foolishness; and my sins are not hid from thee" (Psalm 69:5).

34. "My prayer is unto Thee, O Lord, in an acceptable time. O God, in the multitude of Thy

mercy hear me" (Psalm 69:13).

35. "I will praise the name of God with a song, and will magnify Him with thanksgiving. O Lord, our Lord, how excellent is Thy name in all the earth!" (Psalm 69:30; 8:9).

36. "This is the day which the Lord hath made; we will rejoice and be glad in it" (Psalm 118:24).

Chapter 21
"Promise of Healing"

THE PRAYER OFFERED IN FAITH

The promise of restoration is a journey. Healing may not come easily. There may be deep valleys ahead, through which we must walk.

You will be tempted to give up. You may be following the steps to healing faithfully and still not feel any better about yourself or any closer to the Lord. You may think, *This isn't working. There must be a better way.* When such thoughts come to mind, you can be sure who is placing them there. It is the enemy who has kept you in bondage for so many years. He does not want you to be set free. Make no mistake: Our struggle is not against flesh and blood but against the powers and rulers of darkness.

During times of discouragement at the slow rate of progress, we need to remind ourselves of Paul's words: "We also exult [rejoice] in our tribulations; knowing that tribulation brings about perseverance; and perseverance, proven character; and proven character, hope" (Romans 5:3,4, NASB). During times of discouragement, let us persevere. Let us continue walking down that road of our journey, ever yoked with Him who alone has the power to heal, teach and strengthen us.

During those days of discouragement, let us remember to be thankful: *"Always* giving thanks for *all things* in the name of our Lord Jesus Christ to God even the Father" (Ephesians 5:20, NASB). He will give us hope as He daily works in us to conform us to His image.

Rejoicing, giving thanks and persevering serve to build our faith. The promise of healing is based on faith-our faith in the person of the Lord Jesus Christ: "And without faith it is impossible to please Him, for he who comes to God must believe that He is, and that He is a rewarder of those who seek Him" (Hebrews 11:6, NASB).

Many have been healed because of their faith:

> The blind men came upon Him, and Jesus said to them, "Do you believe that I am able to do this?" They said to Him, "Yes, Lord." Then He touched their eyes, saying, "Be it done to you according to your faith" (Matthew 10:28,29).
>
> "O woman, great is thy faith: be it unto thee even as thou wilt." And her daughter was made whole from that very hour (Matthew 15:28).
>
> And he said to the woman, "Thy faith hath saved thee, go in peace (Luke 7:50).
>
> And he said unto him, "Arise, go thy way: thy faith hath made thee whole" (Luke 17:19).
>
> And Jesus...asked him..."What wilt thou that I shall do unto thee?" And he said, "Lord, that I may receive my sight." And Jesus said unto him, "Receive thy sight; thy faith hath saved thee" (Luke 18:40-42).

146.

As you continually and daily come to Him in prayer, He will build your faith. You will develop a trust relationship deeper than you have ever known before. You will learn the joy of intimate communion with the living, loving God.

As your journey continues, you will look back, from time to time, and see how far you have come. One day you'll notice that the old feelings of rejection just aren't triggered anymore. The pains of interference are gradually disappearing. You may not know exactly when or how, but you will know that you are different. He has been working His transforming work in your life, your emotions and your relationships.

And as long as you continue coming to Him, you can be "confident of this very thing, that He who began a good work in you will perfect it until the day of Christ Jesus" (Philippians 1:6, NASB).

Then you will be able to rejoice with David:

The Lord hath heard my supplication; the Lord will receive my prayer (Psalm 6:9).

O Lord my God, I cried unto thee, and thou hast healed me (Psalm 30:2).

I will bless the Lord at all times: His praise shall continually be in my mouth. (Psalm 34:1).

I will praise thee, O Lord, among the people: I will sing unto thee among the nations (Psalm 57:9).

O clap your hands, all ye people; shout unto God with the voice of triumph (Psalm 47:1).

147.

Chapter 18
"Touched By the Master"

Be Watchful, Be Vigilant

One of the best kept secrets in Christendom is that you and I, because we are Christians, have power and authority over satan. Survey twenty Christians, asking each one individually, "Do you believe in the existence of satan or the devil?" Chances are that nineteen will give you an unequivocal yes, and the twentieth will probably acknowledge his existence but not quite so certainly.

Ask, "Do you know he has power?" and once again you will undoubtedly receive affirmation and agreement.

Next ask, "Do you think he uses or is able to use that power against you?" Now you will probably run into significant doubt and uncertainty in the answers you receive.

And then, Do you think you as an individual have power and authority that exceeds his?" Now the indecision will run deeper!

Finally, ask, "Do you know how to use your authority over him? Have you ever used it?" Many will respond no. After all, if Christians do not really know that satan can attack, interfere with and influence them, is no reason for them to know how to deal with him. He is, for many, a non-issue!

The simple truth is that satan - the prince of

148.

darkness, Lucifer, the devil, apollyon, abaddon or baal, whatever name may be most familiar - has already exerted his controlling influence over any unsuspecting Christians. As a result they are spiritually powerless, ineffective and often defeated.

> *Be on the alert. Your adversary, the*
> *devil, prowls about like a roaring lion,*
> *seeking someone to devour. But resist*
> *him, firm in (my) our faith.* (1Pet. 5:8-9)

It need not be so! We have nothing to fear in satan! Fear comes only when we become slothful and lazy. The Lord Jesus has already given us His power and authority over satan. A fool he is, but he has already been defeated. It remains for us only to exercise the power that is ours by inheritance. Why fear someone over whom you can have immediate control and supremacy? We fear the unknown or the danger confronting us only when we see not alternative or escape. With satan we do not need an escape! We can move in with confidence and clear him out. He is the one who must run. When we move forward against him with determination, poise and conviction, he will flee!

The Word of God gives us all the knowledge we need. "Resist the devil and *he will flee from you!*" HE has no choice. He must flee when we use the spiritual weapons the Lord has already given us. Did the Lord Jesus ever run from the devil or evil spirits? Of course not! Jesus met them head-on and exercised His authority over them, and they obeyed!

149.

Likewise, when we invoke the power Jesus has given us, satan and those who serve him must obey us.

God's Armory

Listen to what God says to us in 2 Corinthians 10: 3-6 (NIV):

1. "For though we live in the world, we do not wage war as the world does."

2. "The weapons we fight with are not the weapons of the world."

3. "On the contrary, they have divine power to demolish strongholds."

4. "We demolish arguments and every pretension that sets itself up against the knowledge of God."

5. "We take captive every thought to make it obedient to Christ."

6. "We will be ready to punish every act of disobedience."

We can glean several insights from this forthright proclamation of the weapons in God's armory.

Line 1: We do not wage war as the world wages war. We already know the outcome; we know who will be the victor. There is no mystery!

Line 2: We have many different weapons available to us, each designed to be uniquely successful in specific situations; we need not use the same weapon for every conflict. Our weapons are not worldly. They do not have to be fired, swung or transported. They require neither basic nor advanced training. We need to know only what weapons are available to us and then go into God's armory to get them.

Line 3: Our weapons have divine power to demolish and destroy strongholds and fortresses the enemy may have erected. These weapons have *power to destroy!* The issue is never in doubt.

Line 4: We will demolish everything the enemy sets up against the knowledge and the truth of God.

Line 5: We are fully armed and equipped spiritually to take captive all servants of the enemy commanding that they become obedient to Christ or suffer the dire consequences of utter defeat.

Line 6: We do not threaten. We are ready, and we *will,* without any hesitation, punish all disobedience!

Our Most Important Weapon

The most valuable and important weapon God has placed in His armory is too seldom used, and for many it lies rusty and neglected. This is the weapon of rebuking, binding and banishing satan. How often do you personally exercise you God-given authority over satan? If you're like most Christians, you seldom, if ever, use this powerful weapon. You will be thrilled and strengthened at the changes that will take place in your life when you begin to throw your spiritual weight and authority around!

First Peter 5: 8-9 tells us, "Be on the alert. Your adversary, the devil, prowls about like a roaring lion, seeking someone to devour. But resist him, firm in your faith." If the Scripture says it so succinctly, why do so many Christians ignore the fact that satan is boldly seeking to devour anyone he can? Though he

151.

prowls about like a roaring lion, he is actually a cowardly pussycat who slinks off into the bulrushes when confronted with strength and authority in the name of the Lord Jesus Christ.

At the same ti
me, satan is also a subtle infiltrator (see Gen. 3:1). He strikes when and where we least expect him. Is that a surprise? He is a liar and   deceiver. He doesn't fight fair. That is why we must be alert and vigilant. We must learn to discern and identify his attacks and interferences for what they are.

Paul told the Corinthians, "I fear...as the serpent beguiled Eve through his subtlety, so your minds should be corrupted." And no wonder, for even satan disguises himself as an angel of light. Therefore it is not surprising if his servants also disguise themselves as servants of righteousness." Scripture, both the New Testament and the Old, is replete with illustrations, admonitions and descriptions exhorting us to be alert. Yet much of the church remains asleep and unaware or, too often, disinterested.

The Authority for Using Our Weapons

Let us look briefly at a few key scriptures.

1. "Then he called his twelve disciples together, and gave them power and authority over all devils."

Here a gift has been given to the twelve. They have received power and authority over all devils.

2. "After this the Lord chose another seventy–two men and sent them out, two by two, to go ahead of him to every town and place where he himself was about to go...the seventy-two men came back in great joy. 'Lord,' they said, 'even the demons obeyed us when we commanded them in your name!'"

Clearly these seventy-two appointees have been given the identical power and authority that was given to the twelve! The gift is no longer limited in scope or bestowal! The Lord has chosen to give it to this additional larger, unnamed, unidentified and apparently insignificant group.

3.   Then Jesus replied to them, "Behold, I give unto you power to tread on serpents (metaphorically satan) and scorpions (evil spirits), and over all the power of the enemy: and nothing shall by any means hurt you...the spirits are subject unto you."

Read that last verse again. It is amazing empowerment that is often overlooked. Simply stated, you and I as Christians have already been given Jesus' power over satan, demonic forces, evil spirits and over "all the power of the enemy." The verse also states that, even though satan has power, we have power *over* his power! Our power is greater than his power, and therefore he is subject to our power when we exercise it. Hence, when we read in James 4:7 to "resist the devil," we are also told, "he will flee from you." He has no choice. He must flee. The roaring lion will slink off into the bulrushes like a whipped pussy cat.

153.

The One Absolute Essential

In our own name or in our own power we have absolutely no authority or power over satan. In fact, if we try to battle him he will laugh and sneer at us and attack us with even more determination because he knows we are not armed. He will see that we are defenseless.

But the moment we invoke Jesus' power, satan becomes defenseless. The power is seen in Luke 10:17: "Lord, even the demons are subject to us *in Your name.*" When you speak to satan or his servants, when you command them in the name of the Lord Jesus Christ, they have no choice but to obey! Try it. If you have never exercised your authority over satan before, you will be amazed at how quickly he flees.

For two reasons, taking authority over satan should always be done aloud. First, Jesus always spoke aloud to him, never silently or under His breath. Scripture records that demons and evil spirits responded to Jesus' audible commands. Second, there seems to be no evidence that satan can read our minds, but there is certain proof that he can hear us. The loudness of your voice is inconsequential. In other words, your authority is not enhanced by shouting. Jesus never did. He simply spoke with authority. You and I can do exactly the same. Our complete and only authority rests in His name.

As you stand and read loud the commandment prayer (page 43, 44) and the prayer of thankfulness, something very significant and discernible may happen. If any emotional struggles were going on

154.

within you such as fear, depression, anger or low self-worth, to name just a few, you will very likely feel that they have lifted or completely disappeared! Why? Because they were simply an attack of the enemy. You have commanded the attacker to leave you. It does not mean that he will not attack again tomorrow. But if he does, you will know how to rebuke him and to resist and "extinguish all the flaming missiles of the evil one."

In the suggested commandment prayer only eight words are absolutely essential. Otherwise you can modify it in any way you feel led by the Spirit to fit your circumstances and need. What are those eight essential words? Repeat them now aloud: "In the name of the Lord Jesus Christ!"

I am convinced that the enemy knows all our weaknesses, our vulnerabilities or, as I call them, our "open windows." He never attacks us in our area of strengths. He attacks only our frailties, especially areas where he has built strongholds and fortresses of the mind.

Long-term freedom from his attacks involves several additional things. First it requires that we find the open windows and shut them. It also requires daily specific prayer for the cleansing and healing of these areas. It requires daily rebuking of the enemy, casting him out of your home, your life and your ministry. It requires your feeling absolutely assured that you do have authority over him and that you have no hesitation to use that power against him!

Some time ago during my daily prayer time (I call it my daily communion with my Lord), I was clearly

155.

directed by the Lord to automatically and regularly rebuke the enemy whether or not I felt attacked. For some reason which I cannot specifically explain, I did this only periodically despite the Lord's direction. I did do it consistently when I felt or knew I was being attacked, and when I perceived any emotional disruption in the promised peace of Jesus. Whenever I did so the bondage, or whatever it was, lifted immediately. The feeling of release is always clear evidence that you were experiencing an attack! And I did pray regularly for discernment so I would quickly recognize any momentary upset or disharmony for what it really was and take the necessary rapid and appropriate response against it.

About two months ago, however, as I was communing with the Lord, He reminded me that He had already directed me to stand against the enemy *daily,* whether or not I thought I was being attacked. I knew I had been gently reprimanded, and this time I took the admonition to heart! Without missing a day, I have stood against the enemy since then. I have the ministries the Lord has given us, from my children's and grandchildren's lives. I wish I could fully describe to you what a change this has made. I wish I could tell you how free from attack both Florence and I have been! I have long recognized that I am the spiritual head of my wife, and therefore I believe it is my spiritual duty to protect her in every way, emotionally, physically and by all means spiritually. By banishing satan from my wife and by standing in front of her with my shield of faith in one hand and my sword in the other, I am fulfilling my scriptural responsibility.

What a change it has made! It has been *incredible.*
There have been no attacks; the windows of vulnerabilities and compulsions the enemy opened in me
many years ago have been securely shut and sealed.
He has not succeeded in opening any at all that I am
aware of. Likewise, things that once might have
bothered Florence and caused consternation for her no
longer do! Despite the stresses and rigors of her life
of ministry and travel, she now sleeps more soundly
than she ever has before!

I will continue my daily banishing and bashing of
the enemy until the Lord tells me it is no longer necessary. I have a feeling I may be waiting for that
message a long time! Why do I share this with you?
Because I strongly encourage you to do the same.
Banish satan daily from your life. You will be just as
thrilled with the results as I have been. A good time
to do it is just before you go to sleep. The enemy
loves to interfere with your sleep.

As the Scripture says, "Now you know this truth;
how happy you will be if you put it into practice!" I
urge you to photocopy the prayer as it appears on
pages 43 and 44 and place the copies in strategic
places as reminders to exercise daily your authority
over satan and over all the powers of the enemy.

It is the same prayer we always pray when we are
praying someone into the presence of the Lord. This
prayer is definitive and final, so we can proceed without his interference. Having said it, you have effectively banished satan in the name of the Lord Jesus.

Remember, the Bible admonishes us to, "Be
watchful, be vigilant"!

Scriptural Authority for Memory Retrieval (Part I)

Joshua 6 & 7   Especially : Chapter 7:13-14, 22

Matthew 13:24-30 Parable of the tares and the wheat
      36-40   ****
      24   God (see v. 37) sowed good seed in His field.
      25   The enemy (the devil, v. 39) sowed tares (weeds) among the wheat. Significance of verses 30-31.

Matthew 15:13   "Every plant which my heavenly Father did not plant shall be rooted up."

John 11:39-41   "Jesus said, 'Remove the stone.' Martha said to Him, 'Lord, by this time there will be a stench.' Jesus said to her...'If you believe you <u>will</u> see the Glory of God.' And so <u>they</u> removed the stone. (NAS)
      44   "Jesus said, 'Unbind him, and let him go.'" (NAS)

II Chron. 29:5 & 16   "Hezekiah said unto them, Hear me, ye Levites, sanctify now yourselves, and sanctify the house of the Lord God of your fathers, and carry forth the filthiness out of the holy place"...
"And the priests went into the inner part of the house of the Lord, to cleanse it, and brought out all the uncleanness that they found in the temple of the Lord. (KJV)

Hebrews 12:1 "Lay aside every encumbrance and the sin which so easily entangles us."

Psalm 31:4 "Free me from the trap that is set for me." (NIV)

Matthew 23:26 "First clean the inside of the cup .... so that the outside of it may become clean also."

1 John 1:9 "If we confess (acknowledge, agree) our sins, He is faithful and just to 1) forgive us our sins (that we commit) and 2) to cleanse us from all unrighteousness (sins committed against us)."

Ezekiel 36:33-36 "This is what the Sovereign Lord says: 'On the day I cleanse you from all your sins, I will resettle your towns, and the ruins will be rebuilt. The desolate land will be cultivated instead of lying desolate in the sight of all who pass through it. They will say, 'This land that was laid waste has become like the garden of Eden; the cities that were lying in ruins, desolate and destroyed, are now fortified and inhabited.' Then the nations around you that remain will know that I the Lord have rebuilt what was destroyed and have replanted what was desolate. I the Lord have spoken, and I will do it." (NIV)

Isaiah 48: 66 I have shown thee new things from this time, even hidden things, and thou didst know them.

159.

Scriptural Authority for Memory Retrieval (Part II)

Psalm 18: 16-19   "He reached down from on high and took hold of me; he drew me out of deep waters. He rescued me from my powerful enemy, from my foes, who were too strong for me. They confronted me in the day of my disaster, but the Lord was my support. He brought me out into a spacious place; he rescued me because he delighted in me."

Psalm 19: 12-13   "Cleanse thou me from hidden (and unconscious) faults (hurts) ...Let them not have dominion over me! (Amplified.)

Psalm 51: 6   "Surely you desire truth in the inner parts; you teach me wisdom in the inmost place."

Psalm 139   "O Lord, you have searched me and you know me. You know when I sit and when I rise; you perceive my thoughts from afar. You discern my going out and my lying down; you are familiar with all my ways. Before a word is on my tongue you know it completely, O Lord." (and continuing to the end)

Matthew 25: 14-30   (The Parable of the Talents)

Psalm 146: 7-8   "He upholds the cause of the oppressed and gives food to the hungry. The Lord sets prisoners free, the Lord gives sight to the blind, the Lord lifts up those who are bowed down, the Lord loves the righteous."

Luke 11: 34   "The lamp of your body is your eye; when your eye is clear (healthy), your whole body also is full of light; but when it is bad, your body also is full of darkness. (NAS)

Luke 12: 2   "There is nothing covered up that will not be revealed, and hidden that will not be known" (Also Matt 10:26 & Mark 4:22) (NAS)

Luke 15:8   "Or what woman, if she has ten silver coins (*or years?*) and loses one coin does not <u>light</u> a lamp and <u>sweep</u> the house and <u>search</u> diligently until she finds it.

I Corinthians 4:5   "...The Lord comes who will...bring to light the things hidden in the darkness." (NAS)

Amos 3:7   "Surely the Lord God will... revealeth His secret unto His servants"

Proverbs 25:2   "It is the glory of God to conceal a thing: but the honor of kings is to search (it) out.

II Corinthians 3:16   "Whenever a man turns to the Lord, the veil is taken away

161.

Possible Blockage to Memory Retrieval or to Seeing Jesus

1. Demonic spirits
2. Fear
3. Denial
4. Protection—fidelity to perpetrator
5. Questioning
6. Lack of Faith (or misplaced trust)
7. Theology
8. Forgiveness
9. God knows we are not ready
10. Garden is not prepared
11. Outside distractions
12. Disassociation
13. Unconfessed sin
14. Drugs, i.e. anti-depressants
15. Prior psychology
16. New Age experience
17. Lies we have believed
18. Lack of emotional desire
19. Rationalization
20. Fear of exposure
21. Generational curses—soul ties
22. Shame feeling from memory retrieval
23. Feeling unworthy
24. Having seen satan masquerading as Jesus
25. Impatience
26. Putting God to the test

TAKING THE SURVEY

Adapted from "Promise of Healing" Chapter 9

Please take the following survey. Simply read over the list. If the statement applies to you or has applied to you at any time in your life—childhood, adolescence, teenage, or young-adult years—put a check on the appropriate line. If it applied when you were a child but no longer does, still put a mark on the line. Leave the line blank if it does not or never did apply. In thousands of applications, this simple test has proven to be better than 99 percent accurate when answered honestly.

Some of you may prefer to have someone else– your spouse or a close friend– read the survey aloud to you as you mark your answers. The results may be surprising. You should take the appropriate survey (for men or women) before reading the explanations that follow the list.

Surveys are adapted from Fred Littauer's *The Promise of Restoration/Healing** (Nashville: Thomas Nelson Publishers, 1994). All rights reserved. This form may be reproduced. (*Note: In 1994, Thomas Nelson Publishers changed the name of the book from *The Promise of Restoration*, originally published by Here's Life Publishers to *The Promise of Healing*.)

MEN'S SURVEY OF EMOTIONS AND EXPERIENCES

PLEASE CHECK EACH LINE THAT APPLIES OR EVER HAS APPLIED
(LEAVE BLANK ANY THAT DO NOT APPLY OR YOU ARE NOT SURE OF)

1. Affairs during marriage .... _____
2. Afraid of big or black dogs.................... _____
3. Alcoholic parent .... _____
4. Being chased in dreams .... _____
5. Brother or sister molested as a child....... _____
6. Candles in dreams .... _____
7. Childhood "bad houses or bad rooms".... _____
8. Childhood depression......................... _____
9. Downcast looks as a child .... _____
10. Dreams of snakes .... _____
11. Early childhood anger .... _____
12. Early childhood masturbation (before 10) _____
13. Emotionally abused as a child .... _____
14. Emotions suppressed in childhood .... _____
15. Fear of being alone .... _____
16. Fear of knives .... _____
17. Feel unworthy of God's love .... _____
18. Feeling "dirty" .... _____
19. Fits of rage .... _____
20. Frequent teenage masturbation .... _____
21. Giving of oral sex repugnant .... _____
22. Guilt feelings .... _____
23. Hate Halloween .... _____
24. Hate homosexuals .... _____
25. Hear chanting or laughing in dreams ...... _____
26. Hide real feelings .... _____
27. Lack of trust .... _____
28. Low self-worth .... _____
29. Marital sexual disinterest .... _____
30. Memory gaps in childhood .... _____
31. Migraine headaches .... _____
32. Obsessive focus on breasts or vagina .... _____
33. Panic attacks .... _____
34. People wearing hoods or robes in dreams.. _____
35. Physically abused as child .... _____
38. Poor teenage relationships with girls...... _____
39. Recurring bad dreams .... _____

38. Rejection feelings .... ____
39. Same sex attraction .... ____
40. Scared by bells, chimes or gongs............ ____
41. Self-hatred .... ____
42. Sexually abused or molested as child...... ____
43. Sexual compulsions, magazines, videos... ____
44. Sometimes hear voices.......................... ____
45. Spiders in dreams .... ____
46. Strange feelings about "the cross".......... ____
47. Struggle with holiness .... ____
48. Suicidal feelings .... ____
49. Teenage promiscuity............................ ____
50. Teenage sexual touching with boys .... ____
51. Temptation to touch children sexually...... ____
52. Tendency to overreact .... ____
53. Tendency to look at others' penises .... ____
54. Uncomfortable with nudity in marriage.... ____
55. Uncontrollable anger .... ____
56. Uncontrollable crying .... ____
57. Undiagnosed pains, aches .... ____
58. Unexplained fear of darkness .... ____

TOTALS ____ ____ ____ ____

         24   11   13   10

GRAND TOTAL _____

1) ____ I have never been in counseling.

2) ____ I have been in counseling for about ____ months, or ____ years.

3) ____ Type: Psychiatric ____; Psychological ____; Marriage/Fam.____

4) The counseling did help ____; or did not particularly help me ____.

5) Basic reason for counseling was _____

   _____

6) Divorced _____   Remarried _____

7) Age _____

WOMEN'S SURVEY OF EMOTIONS AND EXPERIENCES

1. Affairs during marriage .... ____
2. Afraid of big or black dogs.................... ____
3. Alcoholic parent .... ____
4. Anorexia/bulimia .... ____
5. Being chased in dreams .... ____
6. Brother or sister molested as a child....... ____
7. Candles in dreams .... ____
8. Childhood "bad houses or bad rooms".... ____
9. Childhood depression........................ ____
10. Date rape .... ____
11. Dislike roses or their smell .... ____
12. Don't like full moon .... ____
13. Downcast looks as a child .... ____
14. Dreams of snakes .... ____
15. Early childhood anger .... ____
16. Early childhood masturbation (before 10) ____
17. Emotionally abused as a child .... ____
18. Emotions suppressed in childhood .... ____
19. Fear of being alone .... ____
20. Fear of knives .... ____
21. Fear of losing weight .... ____
22. Fear of rape .... ____
23. Feel unworthy of God's love .... ____
24. Feeling "dirty" .... ____
25. Fits of rage ....____
26. Guilt feelings .... ____
27. Hate Halloween .... ____
28. Hate men .... ____
29. Hear chanting or laughing in dreams ...... ____
30. Hide real feelings .... ____
31. Lack of trust .... ____
32. Low self-worth .... ____
33. Marital sexual disinterest .... ____
34. Memory gaps in childhood .... ____
35. Migraine headaches .... ____
36. Panic attacks .... ____
37. People wearing hoods or robes in dreams.. ____

38. PMS/PMT .... ____
39. Poor teenage relationships with boys ...... ____
40. Recurring bad dreams .... ____
41. Rejection feelings .... ____
42. Same sex attraction .... ____
43. Scared by bells, chimes or gongs .... ____
44. Self-hatred .... ____
45. Sexually abused or molested as child ...... ____
46. Sexual compulsions .... ____
47. Sometimes hear voices .... ____
48. Spiders in dreams .... ____
49. Strange feelings about "the cross" .... ____
50. Suicidal feelings .... ____
51. Teenage promiscuity .... ____
52. TMJ .... ____
53. Temptation to touch children sexually ...... ____
54. Uncomfortable with nudity in marriage .... ____
55. Uncontrollable anger .... ____
56. Uncontrollable crying .... ____
57. Undiagnosed pains, aches .... ____
58. Unexplained fear of darkness .... ____

                          TOTALS   ____   ____   ____   ____
                                    21   14   11   12
                     GRAND TOTAL _____

1) ____ I have never been in counseling.

2) ____ I have been in counseling for about ____ months, or ____ years.

3) ____ Type: Psychiatric ____; Psychological ____; Marriage/Fam. ____

4) The counseling did help ____; or did not particularly help me ____.

5) Basic reason for counseling was _____

   _____

6) Divorced _____   Remarried _____

7) Age _____

SCORING THE SURVEY
Adapted From "Get a Life Without the Strife"

Add up your responses in each of the four columns and enter your score on the Totals lines (numbers under each Totals line indicate the possible number for that column). Then add up your four column totals to get your Grand Total of responses.

The first thing to realize in looking at your scores is that every statement on the list is a possible symptom of childhood sexual victimization or interference, with one exception: "Sexually abused or molested as a child" (No. 45 for women, No. 42 for men). It is not a symptom. It is a fact.

The survey, therefore, is simply a list of these symptoms, which lead us to the source. When you go to a medical doctor to find out why you're not feeling well, the first thing he or she does is check for symptoms. When the symptoms are found, the diagnosis can be made and the appropriate remedy or medication prescribed. When your car is sputtering, the first thing a mechanic does is to check for the symptoms. Is there any reason to think it would not be the same with emotional problems? That is why this survey is so effective. As a list of symptoms it quickly leads us to the source of the problem.

Once we have discovered the root, then we can apply the remedy. As you look at your scores (the number of symptoms you have acknowledged about yourself) you may have felt one of the typical reactions listed here. Put a check in front of the one with which you most closely identify.

168.

_____ 1. I've always wondered about that. Maybe now I can get to the bottom of my problem.
_____ 2. Is this possible? I can't believe it could have happened to me.
_____ 3. This is impossible! I was raised in a good Christian home. My father would never have done such a thing.
_____ 4. If it's true, I don't want to know. I'm afraid I couldn't handle it.

Which one is closest to your feelings? The first response is the healthiest. It may be summarized as acceptance; the second, doubt; the third, denial; and the fourth, fear. If you had approximately twelve or more responses on the survey and your response above was number 2, 3, or 4, begin praying for God to remove your doubt, denial, or fear of the possibility.

Remember the statistics:

- **Three out of four women have significant symptoms of victimization.**
- **One out of four acknowledges or is aware of it.**
- **Two out of four have no knowledge of it but do have the symptoms. The violation has been suppressed into the unconscious or unknown.**
- **Six out of ten men have significant symptoms of childhood sexual victimization!**
- **Only one out of ten acknowledges or is aware of it.**
- **Therefore, five out of ten men have the symptoms but have not conscious awareness.**

Responses in the First Column

The first of the four columns, labeled "Clear," is of special significance. This means in our judgment

169.

every statement answered in the first column is a clear symptom of childhood sexual violation. If properly and honestly answered, it can directly and clearly be attributed to no other thing. On this test most people who have in fact been violated, whether known or unknown, will indicate at least four symptoms in this column. Many, however, will make eight, ten, fourteen, or more responses. The following discussion will explain the significance and meaning of these responses. The numbers correspond to the questions on the surveys.

Reponses in the Second and Third Columns

Responses in the second column, labeled "Strong," mean these responses are frequently seen in people who have suffered childhood trauma, but their roots could also be attributed to other sources. They are important, but of lesser significance in getting to the bottom line quickly. The third column, identified as "Possible," shows that these symptoms are still of lesser importance. Their roots are even more apt to have come from nonsexual abuse and usually indicate rejection. However, these symptoms do give an enhanced picture of the overall issues that someone may be facing. (The fourth column, labeled "Group," will be discussed later.)

170.

Analyzing Your First-, Second-, and Third-Column Responses

How many first-column symptoms did you check on the survey? Remember: The symptoms lead us to the general area of the truth. Through memory-retrieval prayer, the Holy Spirit can reveal the exact nature of the truth. If the possibility that you may have been violated is a shock to you, if you want to disbelieve or doubt that it could have happened, then look at some of the other symptoms that you checked in the second and third columns. Why have some of these things been a problem for you? Did you check, perhaps, a total of twenty-four symptoms? You may be able to rationalize two or three of them. But can you explain away every single one of them? Remember that Jesus said, "I have come that they may have life, and that they may have it more abundantly" (John 10:10). You may have eternal life, but is your life here on earth abundant? If your answer is no, then perhaps it is time to open your mind to the fact that there must be a reason why you checked so many symptoms. Acceptance is the first step on the healing journey!

Responses in the Fourth-Column (Group Symptoms)

The fourth column on both forms of the survey is used to indicate "group symptoms." Your marks in this column may be an indication that when violation occurred, it could have been by a number of perpetrators, or a group, rather then a single violator.

If you checked several of the fourth-column symptoms, you have most likely checked many in the first three columns as well. Generally, people who have checked five or six in the fourth column will have checked ten or more in the first column. They are also apt to have a grand total of about thirty-five (35) or more responses. The symptoms in the fourth column indicate an even more traumatic form of victimization.

SUMMARY OF GENERAL PRINCIPLES RELATING TO VICTIMS OF CHILDHOOD SEXUAL INTERFERENCE

1. An emotionally healthy person is rarely attracted to an emotionally unhealthy person.
2. Our emotions remember what our minds have forgotten.
3. Awareness of interference is the first step to freedom.
4. Interference is significantly more prevalent in families with strict attitudes against family nudity.
5. Absence of memory does not indicate absence of violation.
6. Sexual interference distorts and disrupts the normal and natural sexual development of a boy or girl.
7. Sexual interference destroys or weakens a child's natural defenses against later inappropriate sexual contact.
8. Sexual interference is the result, not the cause, of a breakdown in a family.
9. A child is not created by God with prevailing feelings of anger, rejection, hate or depression.
10. Gaps in childhood memory are a significant indication that a child's body and emotions were probably defiled by sexual trauma.
11. Eyes are the mirror of the soul. Sparkle reflects joy and serenity reflects inner peace. Sexual trauma is frequently reflected by pain, deadness, fear or intensity.
12. Release from inner turmoil comes with recognizetion, and restoration comes with the Redeemer.

13. Jesus Christ is faithful and just to cleanse us from the sins that were committed against us (1 John 1:9).
14. Virtually all victims of childhood sexual interference have low self-esteem. They feel dirty, unwanted, used or unlovable.
15. Unexplained feelings or hatred, anger, fear or stress are an almost certain symptom of sexual interference.
16. Intellectual assent to forgiveness is often ineffective when the victim does not know what or why he or she is forgiving.
17. When several siblings show symptoms or instability, the interference will tend to be found within the family structure.
18. People tend to marry on similar levels of pain, even when the trauma is unknown. Victims usually marry victims.
19. The dogmatically protective parent and the reactionary spouse may be hiding their own perversions, guilt or childhood trauma.
20. The energy required to maintain suppression of traumatic pain drains the individual, often resulting in passivity, depression and defeat (see Psalm 32:46, NIV).
21. The spouse of a victim becomes the secondary victim and may take on symptoms such as guilt and anger transmitted by the emotions of the victim.
22. "Deliverance" experiences that do not deal with the repressed trauma are apt to amplify the shame,

guilt, discouragement and resignation when the victim finds the symptoms recurring.

23. Victims are often not content at doing what they are good at and are apt to blunder in areas in which they are not qualified.

24. Satan is always on the prowl, ready to reopen the healed-over areas of hurt and pain.

25. The victim personality accepts abuse as a normal way of life.

26. The victim personality is often unable to see the truth about himself or herself.

27. Adult uncontrollable anger is usually the result of the sins and hurts that were committed against the child.

NOTES

Chapter One
"The Throne"

1. See Luke 12:34, NIV
2. See Matthew 6:24, NLT
3. See Matthew 23: 25-26, NIV
4. See Mark 7: 20-23, NIV
5. See Psalm 19:12, NIV
6. See Hebrews 13:21, NIT

Chapter Two
"Getting Fully Dressed"

1. See Ephesians 6:13-17, NIV
2. See Isaiah 32:17, NIV
3. See John 8:32, NIV
4. Luke 1:79, NKJV
5. See Psalm 149:4, NIV
6. See Hebrews 4:12, NIV
7. See 1 Corinthians 16:13, NIV
8. Ephesians 6: 11-12, NKJV
9. "The Armor of God" Prayer, *Promise of Healing Workshop*, page 27
   Look up these scriptures for added support:
   Isaiah 52:12
   Isaiah 59:17
   II Samuel 22:33
   Psalm 28
   Hebrews 4:12
   II Corinthians 10:4
   Romans 8:37

10. No, the small *s* on satan is not a typographical mistake. Although a capital letter is proper English form, it is also a sign of honor and respect, and he doesn't deserve any! Notes Section, *Touched By The Master*, page 211.

Chapter Three
"Tools for Your Tool Belt"

"Name of Jesus"

1. See Philippians 2:10-11, NIV
2. See James 4:7, NLT
3. Suggested Prayer to Rebuke satan and Cast Him Out. *Promise of Healing Workshop*, page 3.

"Cross of Christ"

1. Colossians 2:15, NIV
2. 1 Corinthians 1:18, NIV

"Blood of Christ"

1. Hebrews 9: 14, NKJV

"Scrubbing It All Away"

1. 1 Peter 1:13, NIV
2. Psalm 17: 6, NIV
3. Philippians 4: 6-7
3. John 14: 21, NIV

Chapter Four
"Taking Out the Trash"

"Forgiveness"

1. Ecclesiastes 3: 6-7, NLT
2. Matthew 6: 14-15, NIV
3. "Prayer of Forgiveness", *Promise of Healing Workshop*, page 49.
4. Joshua 24: 15, NLT

"Strongholds and Soul Ties"

1. "What is a Stronghold?" *Touched By The Master,* Chapter 18.
2. "What is a Soul Tie?" *Touched By The Master,* Chapter 18.
3. "How do we Break a Strong Hold," *Touched By The Master,* Chapter 18.
2. Quote Dr. Neil Anderson, *Released From Bondage*, *Promise of Healing Workshop*, page 49.

"Bitter-Root Judgments and Expectancies"

1. Matthew 7: 1-2, Amplified
2. Galatians 6: 7-8, NIV
3. Hebrews 12: 15, NIV
4. Ephesians 6: 2-3, NIV

5. Story of Sarah is a true story but the name has been changed.
6. John 20: 23, NIV
7. "Bitter Root Judgments" adapted from _The Transformation of the Inner Man_, Chapter 14.
8. "Prayer to Break Bitter Root Judgments and Vows", adapted from Stronghold and Soul Tie Prayer, _Touched by the Master_, Chapter 18.
9. Quote Dr. Neil Anderson, _Released From Bondage_, _Promise of Healing Workshop_, page 49.

"The Clutter of Inner Vows"

1. "Prayer for Bitter Root Judgments and Vows", adapted from Stronghold and Soul Tie Prayer, _Touched by the Master_, Chapter 18

2. Look especially for ways you have held bitterness against your Heavenly Father or have judged Him because He did not let you have your way. These bitter-root judgments are what keep us from an intimate relationship with Him and need to be confessed so we can know Him as closely as we know the Son. If you hold bitterness toward Him, it is hard to draw close.

Chapter Five
"Memory Boxes"

1. Romans 12:2, NIV
2. Luke 2:51, NIV
3. 1 Corinthians 4:5, NIV
4. Psalm 119: 105, NLT
5. Romans 12: 1, Message
6. 2 Corinthians 1:3-4, NIV
7. Hebrews 4:13, NIV
8. Psalm 139: 11-12, NIV
9. Ephesians 3:16-19, NIV
10. John 8:36, NIV
11. 2 Corinthians 4:6, NIV
12. Psalm 145: 5, NIV

Chapter Six
"Remodeling With a Pro"

1. Ephesians 5: 13, NIV
2. Matthew 12: 20, NIV
3. Isaiah 58: 12, NIV
4. Hebrews 4: 16, NIV
5. Luke 12: 2, NIV
6. Jeremiah 17: 14, NIV
7. 2 Corinthians 1: 3-4, NIV.

Chapter 18
Touched by the Master
Footnotes

1. James 4:7, emphasis added.
2. 2 Cor. 11:3, KJV.
3. 2 Cor. 11:14-15.
4. Luke 9: 1, KJV.
5. Note that some early writings and today's transla-tions refer to the sending out of "seventy others." There is valid mathematical reason to conclude that the correct figure is actually seventy-two. Luke 9:1 says twelve were sent out; Luke 10:1 says the Lord "appointed seventy-two others." The two groups total eighty-four are seven and twelve, significant numbers in Scripture, repre-senting perfection and administration or comple-tion.
6. Luke 10: 1, 17, TEV.
7. Luke 10: 19-20, KJV.
8. Eph. 6:16.
9. See John 14:27
10. I clearly differentiate here between the spiritual head and the domestic authority in the home. I strongly believe that only the Lord Jesus can be the authority in the home, and therefore the husband cannot be. Nor can the wife. We are to be one, just as we are one in Christ. For further understanding and scriptural perspectives, see chapter 13, "How Can the Husband Be the Head of the Wife?" in my book *Wake Wake Up, Men!*

(Dallas, Tex.: Word, 1994). I hope you will find it interesting and challenging - but I warn you: it *is* different!

11. John 13:17, TEV.

Profits earned from the sales of this book will be used by Shepherd's Heart Ministry, a 501-C3 Not-For-Profit Organization, to provide scholarships for those needing prayer counseling.

Bibliography

Chambers, Oswald, My Utmost for His Highest,.
    London: Dodd, Mead and Co., 1985;
    Westwood, N.J., 1987

Friesen, James G., Ph.D. The Life Model, Living
    From the Heart Jesus Gave You, Shepherd's
    House Ministry, VanNeys, CA, 2000

Littauer, Fred. The Promise of Healing, Nashville:
    Thomas Nelson, 1994

Littauer, Fred. Touched By The Master—the Miracle
    Healing Power of Seeing Jesus, Creation
    House Publ., Orlando, Florida, 1996

Littauer, Fred and Florence, Freeing Your Mind
    From Memories That Bind, San Bernardino,
    Calif.; Here's Life, 1989.

Littauer Fred and Florence. Get a Life Without the
    Strife, Thomas Nelson Publishers, Nashville,
    1993

Littauer, Fred and Florence. The Promise of Healing
    A Prayer Workshop. San Marcos, Calif., THE
    PROMISE OF HEALING, 1992

Sandford, John and Paula. The Transformation of the
Inner Man, Victory House, Inc., Tulsa, OK, 1982

Shepherd's Heart Ministry

This ministry was established in 1999 after having been mentored for two years by Fred Littauer. It was his desire that we carry on the work he did so well with his "Promise of Healing Workshops" and individual prayer sessions. In wearing his mantle of healing the wounded we have used all of the tools in this book with our clients to find the same results he did for many years.

In the ensuing years our staff has also been trained as Theophostic Prayer ministers. Much of what Fred was doing was very similar to this unique program. You will find so many of his experiences he wrote about in "Touched by the Master", only verify the wonderful work that Theophostics is doing in the body of Christ today. All of us have lie based thinking that continues to cripple not only our relationship with others but also our relationship with the church and our God.

It is the continued goal of this ministry to help others find the truth, which is Jesus, that will set them free. We pray that this book will do what Fred hoped all of his work would do which was to till the ground around our lies and our old wounds so the Lord Jesus Christ could easily pull up the root of our pain. We hope this book and the wonderful tools Fred developed in his years of healing work for his own growth and the growth of others will help you to start tilling. If we can help you in anyway at Shepherd's Heart Ministry to use the tool or do some tilling please contact us.

Contact Information

For information on ordering Fred and Florence
Littauer's books contact:

CLASServices, Inc.
Web site: www.classsevices.com
Phone 505.292.5886 or 800.433.6633

You may order "Touched by the Master" on line

To contact Shepherd's Heart Ministry for copies
of this book or for information on our prayer
counseling services write us at:

Shepherd's Heart Ministry
P.O. Box 712
Topeka, KS 66601

Or call us at
Phone 785.233.7214

Profits earned from the sales of this book will be
used by Shepherd's Heart Ministry,
a 501-C3 Not-For-Profit Organization,
to provide scholarships for those needing
prayer counseling.

10795482R10106

Made in the USA
Charleston, SC
05 January 2012